The
Gardens of Wales

Helena Attlee

Photographs by
Alex Ramsay

The
Gardens of Wales

F

FRANCES LINCOLN LIMITED
PUBLISHERS

Frances Lincoln Limited
4 Torriano Mews
Torriano Avenue
London NW5 2RZ
www.franceslincoln.com

British Library Cataloguing in Publication Data
A catalogue record for this book is available from the British Library.

ISBN 978-0-7112-2882-5

Printed in Singapore

9 8 7 6 5 4 3 2 1

HALF TITLE PAGE The Lime Avenue at
Chirk Castle in Clwyd was planted in
the late seventeenth century. The
lead statue is a copy of the Farnese
Hercules, made in the workshop of
John van Nost the Elder. It originally
stood on the north side of the castle.

TITLE PAGE The Orangery and Aviary
Terraces at Powis Castle in Powys.

RIGHT A peacock in the garden of
Llanfihangel Court in Monmouthshire.

contents

20 miles
20 km

LIVERPOOL

Amlwch

A5025

Anglesey

Holyhead

Llangefni

Bodysgallen Hall

Prestatyn

Llandudno
Colwyn
Bay
Rhyl

A548

Bodrhyddan Hall

Menai
Bridge
Bangor

A5

Conwy

Holywell

Flint

Chester

Bodnant

Denbigh

A525

Mold

A494

A55

Plas Newydd

**Crug Farm
Plants**

Caernarfon

A487

A5

A470

Ruthin

Wrexham

A483

Ruabon

A525

Erddig

A487

A470

A494

Porthmadog

Plas Brondanw

A5

Llangollen

A5

Chirk Castle

Criccieth

A497

A470

Oswestry

Pwllheli

A496

A483

Plas-yn-Rhiw

A470

Shrewsbury

A458

A487

A493

Powis Castle

Welshpool

*Cardigan
Bay*

A470

A483

Montgomery

Newtown

A487

Aberystwyth

A470

A483

Knighton

A44

A488

Presteigne

A485

Llandrindod
Wells

A483

A44

Llanllyr

Tregaron

A481

Cae Hir

Lampeter

Builth Wells

A483

A438

Hay-on-Wye

Cardigan

A485

A482

Llandovery

A470

Llowes Court

**Cilwendeg Shell House
Rhos-y-gilwen Mansion**
Fynone

Newcastle
Emlyn

Brecon

A40

A479

A487

Fishguard

A40

Carmarthen

A40

*Llanfihangel
Court*

Haverfordwest

A40

Narberth

A40

A4067

Crickhowell

A40

A478

**Aberglasney
Gardens**

Penpergwm Lodge

Milford
Haven

A4076

Picton Castle

A48

A483

Abergavenny

*Clytha
Park*

Monmouth

Neyland

A477

**National Botanic
Garden of Wales**

Ammanford

Ebbw Vale

Llanover House

*High
Glanau
Manor*

Pembroke

Tenby

A477

Kidwelly

Merthyr
Tydfil

Pontypool

A470

Llanelli

M4

A465

Aberdare

Veddw House

*Wyndcliffe
Court*

Neath

A470

Chepstow

Dewstow Grotto

M48

Swansea
Port
Talbot

Pontypridd

Caerphilly

M4

Newport

M4

Porthcawl

Bridgend

CARDIFF

BRISTOL

Dyffryn Gardens

Barry

Bristol Channel

©Maps in Minutes™/Collins Bartholomew (2007)

introduction

There is no such thing as a typical Welsh garden. The gardens of Wales are as varied as its geography, geology, economy and climate, and as diverse as the people who inhabit it. There are world-famous landscapes such as Powis Castle in mid-Wales and Bodnant in the north, and fascinating, private gardens such as Llowes Court near Hay-on-Wye, which opens only for the National Garden Scheme. The history of some Welsh gardens is obscure, but others are the well-documented work of renowned designers and architects such as Humphry Repton or H. Avray Tipping. *The Gardens of Wales* is a celebration of this wonderful diversity, and it encompasses an enormous range of gardens. There is the modern, conceptual garden at Veddw House near Chepstow, for example, and there are gardens built in the Italianate style of the Arts and Crafts movement, like Plas Brondanw in Gwynedd. There is a fully functioning, Victorian kitchen garden at Rhos-y-Gilwen Mansion in Pembrokeshire, and at Bodysgallen Hall near Llandudno there are the remains of an Elizabethan terrace garden.

When Daniel Defoe travelled through north Wales during the 1720s, he compared its mountains to the Alps, but defied 'even Hannibal himself' to march his army 'over Snowden [sic], or over the rocks of Merioneth and Montgomery Shires'. But although mountains gave Defoe and his contemporaries the horrors, by the end of the eighteenth century Humphry Repton was remodelling the landscape of Plas Newydd on Anglesey to frame the view over the Menai Strait to Snowdonia. What would Defoe have thought of this, or of the indomitable Keating sisters from Nottingham, who selected the Lleyn Peninsula as their home, and made a garden overlooking Hell Bay and the mountains of Merioneth?

In north Wales acid soils combine with a climate tempered by the Gulf Stream, creating ideal conditions for the rhododendrons, azaleas and other ericaceous plants that paint the sides of Bodnant's dell with vivid colour each spring. The effect of the Gulf Stream persists on the coast of west Wales, where Earl Lloyd George has spent the past twenty years building up a collection of over six hundred hardy and tender rhododendrons in his north Pembrokeshire garden at Ffynone.

Some people hate rhododendrons, and that's all right because there is much to interest the plantsman in gardens all over Wales. The National Botanic Garden of Wales in Carmarthenshire was the first new botanic garden to be built in Britain for two hundred years. Norman Foster's Great Glass House was designed to shelter a collection of Mediterranean-climate plants from both hemispheres, and in the Double Walled Garden a new tropical glasshouse has recently opened. Elsewhere, gardeners rejoice in rainfall that exceeds the national average. At Dyffryn, outside Cardiff, Reginald Cory once assembled one of the finest plant collections in Britain, and the magnificent herbaceous borders are still enriched with unusual shrubs such as pineapple guava (*Acca sellowiana*) and loquats (*Eriobotrya japonica*). At Cae Hir, in Ceredigion, a Dutchman creates striking combinations of cultivated and wild plants and, down the road at Llanllyr, the banks of Robert and Loveday Gee's new pond are packed with a rainbow collection of candelabra primulas each spring. Wales also has some outstanding plant nurseries. The most important of these is probably Crûg Farm in Gwynedd, which specializes in unusual herbaceous perennials, shrubs and climbers. Crûg Farm belongs to Sue and Bleddyn Wynn-Jones, who have propagated many of the plants in the nursery from seed that they have collected in remote corners of the Far East and Central America.

Daniel Defoe's journey took him all over Wales. As he progressed southwards to the Borders, he did not entirely escape the mountainous views that he considered 'so horrid and frightful', but he did find 'the people of this county more civiliz'd and more curteous, than in the more mountainous parts, where the disposition of the inhabitants seems to be rough, like the country'. Several of the gardens in this book lie on the Welsh Borders, where individuality is the only unifying theme.

Wales has its share of follies. There is the fabulous and recently restored Cilwendeg Shell House at in Pembrokeshire, the castle at Clytha Park near Abergavenny and Bodnant's Pin Mill. Everybody loves a garden that has been lost and found. Aberglasney in Carmarthenshire is one of Britain's most successful and best-publicized garden rescue stories, but few people know about the underground grotto gardens that have been rediscovered at Dewstow in Monmouthshire.

The gardens in the book are arranged in their counties. The old county names, which are still in general use in Wales, have been given as part of each address in the list of gardens to visit on page 127. Every garden in the book is marked on the map of Wales opposite.

gwynedd

plas brondanw
merionethshire

Sir Clough Williams-Ellis is best known for Portmeirion, a pastiche of a Riviera town in miniature that was built on a wooded promontory on the coast of Snowdonia. He awarded himself the enviable title 'Architect Errant', and in that frivolous place, where architectural fragments merge to create wonderfully fanciful effects, the title seems entirely fitting. In the garden of his family home at Plas Brondanw, however, Sir Clough showed an entirely different side of his nature. Here he worked with the sobriety of a classical Italian architect to create a garden that combines beauty and gravitas in equal measure.

When Sir Clough inherited the Plas Brondanw estate in 1908, the house had been abandoned by his family for many years. Sir Clough was working as an architect in London, so he could not move in. However, he was soon dedicating his energies to what he described as the estate's 'rehabilitation', a process that 'gradually and slowly . . . became my chief absorbing interest outside my profession'. He was, if anything, most passionate about the garden.

> It was for its sake that I worked and stinted, for its sake that I chiefly hoped to prosper. A cheque for ten pounds would come in and I would order yew hedging to that extent, and cheque for twenty and I would pave a further piece of terrace.

The site itself was not particularly large, but all the features surrounding it were on a vast scale. First there was the house, a huge and rugged, four-storey stone building at the top of the slope, and then there was the mountainous landscape on all sides. Sir Clough's response to this grand scale was a layout of the utmost simplicity. He quartered the site with a grid of axes that frame the mountain views from a variety of different points in the garden, drawing them to its heart. The first of these axes was marked by a terrace in front of the house, paved, if Sir Clough is to be believed, in twenty-pound stretches. At its north-eastern end he made a belvedere, with the peak of Cnicht as its focus. In August the terrace is lined on one side by a dark, yew hedge and on the other by an incandescent blaze of white Japanese anemones.

BELOW LEFT Plas Brondanw is designed around views. This circular, raised terrace beneath the holm oak at the centre of the main lawn is slightly reminiscent of a bandstand. It was built to create a dramatic vista of the summit of Cnicht, seen above the neat topiary shapes of the garden's boundary hedge. Clough used the motif of the flaming urn in the foreground throughout the garden.

BELOW RIGHT Looking northwards from the garden to the south of the house, where the main vista is flanked by yews. The strange little figure of a child in a fireman's helmet greets visitors as they enter the garden. His hose, somewhat erratically fed by a natural spring, sprays water into a lily pond at his feet.

ON PAGES 12–13 Looking east across the garden towards the orangery. Plas Brondanw was not conceived as a flower garden, and it is hedges and topiary that hold the whole design together, concealing and then revealing statues, rooflines and distant mountain views.

ABOVE The garden is richly
furnished with statues.
This theatre stands at the end
of a grassy walk to the south of
the house.

The house is linked to the sloping lawn by two sets of curved steps designed to a pattern that might have been taken from Bramante's Cortile del Belvedere in Rome, or even the Temple of Fortune at Praeneste. Sight lines lead across the lawn to the ancient holm oak at its centre, and beyond it to the peak of Meol Hebog. In 1912, Sir Clough built a stone orangery at the southern end of the lawn, creating another axis between it and a *claire-voyée* at its far end that frames a mountain view.

The axes in front of the house lead across the empty lawn towards their distant focus. To the south of the building Sir Clough added more detail to the design. Here the main axis is flanked by yews or pleached limes and lined by a series of enclosed garden rooms. The rooms are densely furnished with plants, urns, statues and pedestals that lead the eye away from the main axis to the views on either side of it.

Russell Sharp, head and only gardener, tends this complex landscape alone. He was head gardener at Portmeirion for many years, and this little place is his retirement project. When he took the garden on, it had been untended for two years. He makes no pretence that it is as tidy as it should be. Fortunately, he is a phlegmatic man with a career's worth of experience and an insatiable appetite for challenges. 'I've got a five-year plan for the hedges,' he tells me. And perhaps he is right, for it is really the architecture, hard and soft, that holds the design together. Sir Clough's vision for the site was so powerful and so successful that a few untidy flowerbeds do nothing to diminish its impact.

ABOVE The terrace in front of the
house is flanked by yew hedges
underplanted with Japanese
anemones that flower in August.
The view is stopped by the belfry
of Sir Clough's elegant garage,
which is now being converted
into a tearoom.

bodysgallen hall
caernarfonshire

Bodysgallen Hall and its gardens have developed in tandem over hundreds of years. The core of the building is a thirteenth-century watchtower built to overlook Conwy Castle. This very practical function had a delightful result for, although the house grew with every century, the extraordinary views of Conwy Castle and Snowdonia remain the same. Bodysgallen was associated with the Mostyn family from the sixteenth century until 1969, when it was sold after the death of Ievan Mostyn. The seventeenth century saw the development of a series of sheltered terraces and small compartments on the steep slope to the south-east of the house. This is the site of a lovely, walled parterre garden and a viewing space above it. The parterre beds are packed with herbs, their scent trapped and amplified by the Elizabethan walls. The parterre itself is not original: it was probably designed in the late nineteenth century by Lady Augusta Mostyn, one of the most important figures in the history of the garden. However, Richard Haslam, in the *Journal of Garden History* (34:1, 2006), describes the layout of this area as 'a vivid example of Renaissance garden structure'. He also presents the garden as an example of the Italianate style brought back to Wales by merchants and sailors during the fifteenth and sixteenth centuries.

A report in the Flintshire County Record Office describes Bodysgallen's gardens in 1854, when the house was 'surrounded by kitchen and flower gardens, shrubbery, walks, a most beautiful terrace and fine old woods and plantations, from many points of which are obtained views of great extent and variety'. The walks, leading to outlying shrubberies and orchards, the croquet lawn and the woods, are still among Bodygallen's greatest charms.

By 1886 Lady Augusta Mostyn had transformed the house once again, adding a new drawing room and dining room, and renovating the entire building in the Arts and Crafts style. In the garden she built a lily pond on the terrace below the south side of the house, and transformed the walled orchard into a rose garden that she gave to her son as a wedding present.

Ievan Mostyn was the last member of the family to live at Bodysgallen. He is said to have been renowned for eccentricities that included a peculiar enthusiasm for shoes and an insatiable desire to travel. Local people still remember going to Bodysgallen as children to ask if they could play football in the walled rose garden – the only level ground in the area. Lord Mostyn always gave his permission, but at six o'clock he would come out on to the terrace and fire a shotgun into the air, sending the children scurrying away.

During Lord Mostyn's lifetime Bodysgallen and its garden fell into a state of gentle dereliction, a process that was not reversed until 1980, when Historic House Hotels bought the house. Happily, the company recognizes the charm of filling the hotel with flowers grown in the walled kitchen garden, and of serving some of the fruit and vegetables that also grow there. As a result John Dennis, head gardener, works much like his Victorian predecessors in a walled garden that is intensively cultivated to produce cutting flowers, soft fruit and vegetables.

BELOW The herb parterre that was probably designed by Lady Augusta Mostyn in the nineteenth century. However, the walls surrounding the parterre were built c.1580, and the garden can be seen from a purpose-built viewing gallery of the same date.

plas yn rhiw
lleyn peninsula

Plas yn Rhiw is a pleasant, stone house tucked into the side of a hill. A sloping, slate porch runs along the seaward side of it, and trees frame a view across the graceful curve of Hell Bay to the mountains of Merioneth. On a clear day the view from the upstairs windows expands to encompass Cardigan Bay and even St David's Head and the islands off the coast of Pembrokeshire. The landscape surrounding the house is windswept, but Plas yn Rhiw and its garden are protected to the north and east by the hill and the trees that grow on it. Its sheltered, south-facing site makes an oasis of the place. Clough Williams-Ellis, architect and owner of the magnificent garden at Plas Brondanw, described this happy setting in the following terms:

To those sailing bleakly across Hell's Mouth … there is just one spot where the eye may gratefully rest on relative 'snugness' and that is where the wooded policies of Plas yn Rhiw meet the sea in a little bay. Here, sheltered by the shoulder of its protecting mountain from the tempestuous west, crouches an ancient manor house – mostly seventeenth-century, with a fashionable Regency facelift.

The house was part of a thriving estate built up by the Lewis family, and owned by them until the last descendant died in 1874 and the estate was divided and sold. Plas yn Rhiw was then bought by Mr Roberts, who lived there with his family until his death. Thereafter house and land were let, and this marked the beginning of a slow decline.

Lorna, Eileen and Honor Keating began to take holidays on the Lleyn Peninsula in 1919. It was during that first summer that they saw Plas yn Rhiw. By this time it was uninhabited and the garden, with its box hedges and narrow paths, was rapidly becoming overgrown. The Keatings returned to the area each summer. They undoubtedly kept an eye on the house, but it lay abandoned for twenty years before coming on to the market in 1939, for only the second time in its long history. The windows were broken, the floorboards rotten and the garden so overgrown that the Keating sisters were forced to clamber in through a first-floor window to view the house. Undaunted, they bought it with, as Honor Keating was to write in her guidebook to the property, an express desire to 'save a unique area of natural beauty to give to the National Trust in memory of their parents'.

Their vision extended beyond the house and the 58 acres/23.5 hectares that came with it: they were determined to give the National Trust the land that had originally belonged to the estate. To this end they spent thirty years buying up little parcels of land whenever they came on the market. They eventually owned 400 acres/162 hectares of coastline, again bought with the sole purpose of preserving its beauty and donating it to the Trust.

It took the builders a year to renovate the house and to install such luxuries as a bathroom and a boiler. Only then did the sisters turn their attention to the garden. Under the brambles they discovered a network of box-lined paths and flowerbeds, and a box parterre on the terrace immediately below the house. Once the ground was cleared, replanting could begin. The sisters worked together in the garden, although Honor is said to have done much of the planting. She took advantage of the sheltered position and the mild climate, combining traditional, cottage garden plants with more unusual or tender species such as the Chilean firebush (*Embothrium coccineum*), *Desfontainia spinosa*, eucryphias, crinodendrons, daphnes and the Chilean bellflower (*Lapageria rosea*). In 1949 she planted the magnificent *Magnolia campbellii* subsp. *mollicomata* that still grows beside the parterre, to mark the end of the war.

The Keatings began negotiations with the National Trust in 1952, but the Trust did not take over management of the garden until the last sister died in 1981. Lorna was ninety by the time of her death, and had lived alone for some years. It's no surprise, then, that the garden was rather overgrown. The Trust has been careful to preserve the relaxed and very private atmosphere of the place. The garden is still a little overgrown, a little shambolic, but

BELOW The view from the upstairs windows of the house extends across the bay to the mountains of Merioneth. The garden's box parterre was already there when the Keatings arrived. Corrine Price, head gardener, suggests that it might have been planted by Lady Strickland, who spent each summer in the house at the beginning of the twentieth century

BELOW LEFT The gardeners deliberately allow plants and even weeds to grow between the cobbles in this courtyard beside the house, as a more formal approach to maintenance would not be in keeping with the garden's past history.

BELOW RIGHT Parts of the house seem to be almost buried in the foliage of plants and trees that thrive in the garden's warm microclimate.

BELOW The rust-red flower of an
Abutilon x *hybridum* 'Ashford Red'
growing through the delicate leaves
of a jasmine in the shelter of the
porch on the seaward side of
the house

'That's what we like,' explains Corinne Price, head gardener and administrator; 'that's what makes it unique.' Since her arrival three years ago, Corinne has undertaken a thinning programme. 'A lot of the plants were overgrowing the hedges,' she explains; 'some of the hedges were damaged, and some had already been lost altogether.' She describes this process as 'a voyage of discovery' that allowed her to uncover plants that had not been seen in the garden for years. Some of these would have been planted by the Keatings, but others were introduced when the National Trust took the garden over in 1981. Among the unexpected treasures were a single *Watsonia meriania* and a *Buddleja colvilei*. 'It's not just about preserving the past,' Corinne explains: 'the Keatings were very interested in finding new plants, and I think they would have been horrified if we hadn't brought in any novelties.' Corinne is also aware of the need to 'move with the times' by, for example, choosing plants suited to the changes in our climate. The garden is managed entirely organically, and this restricts some of her choices. She would like to build up the rose stock, selecting the old English roses and Moss roses that the Keatings are known to have grown, but the old roses don't have much resistance to disease. The 'Zéphirine Drouhin' roses that the Keatings planted to scale the pillars of the porch are still there. 'They are a nightmare for disease,' Corinne says, 'but we won't get rid of them and we won't spray them, so we'll just have to live with it.' All strength to her arm.

plas newydd
anglesey

When Humphry Repton took the landscape at Plas Newydd in hand in 1799, he arranged a stand of beech trees to frame visitors' first view of the house. Today the impact of this view is as powerful as ever. Most of the towering beeches are still there, with the house nestling in a house-sized hollow at the foot of the slope. Nothing interferes with this simple layout. Beyond the trees, smooth, sloping lawns tumble, uninterrupted, to the sea wall, claiming the water in the Menai Strait as their own. Beyond the Strait, which changes constantly with tide, wind and weather, Snowdon and its foothills create yet more drama.

Repton was called to Plas Newydd just after James Wyatt had remodelled the house with Joseph Potter, his assistant. He was unimpressed by the modernization of the grounds, where 'they have proceeded too hastily … in grubbing hedges and pulling down cottages'. His solution was to plant stands of oaks, sycamores and beeches that would 'soften a bleak country, and shelter the ground from violent winds'. His great achievement was providing shelter from the prevailing south-westerly winds, while preserving the unique and heart-meltingly beautiful views across the water.

The Marquesses of Anglesey have worked consistently to enrich the planting of Plas Newydd, but they have achieved their aim without spoiling the wonderful, open nature of the site. Repton's entirely naturalistic landscape was preserved until the end of the nineteenth century, when the 6th Marquess created a small formal garden to the north-east of the house. He continued to develop the rest of the site and, just before the First World War, he began to enrich the woods that flank the lawn to the south of the house by planting evergreen trees such as Monterey cypresses (*Cupressus macrocarpa*) and Scots pines (*Pinus sylvestris*). The 7th Marquess continued his father's tradition, and today the area, known for some reason as the West Indies, is rich with ornamental cherries, camellias, magnolias, maples (*Acer* spp.) and the Chilean firebush (*Embothrium coccineum*). In April the air is heavy with the scent of the *Osmanthus delavayi* that is planted as a hedge, and in May massed plantings of deciduous azaleas fill the space with colour and scent. In mid-summer great drifts of hydrangeas planted by the 7th Marquess flank and punctuate the lawns.

When John Dennis came to Plas Newydd as head gardener in 1979, Lord Anglesey, the 7th Marquess, had given the property to the National Trust only three years before. Lord Anglesey continues to live in the house, however, and thirty years on, his involvement in the garden is undiminished; it is an important part of John Dennis's job to interpret, develop and realize his ideas. It is this collaboration that gives the garden its vibrancy, preventing it from taking on the atmosphere of an institution.

They have worked together particularly closely on the formal terraces to the north-east of the house. Today the terraces, loud with the sound of running water and packed with bold, colourful planting, serve as a perfect foil to the relaxed informality of the woodland gardens and lawns. When John first arrived, the terraces, built by Lord Anglesey's father in 1922, had been neglected. 'He told me that this part of the garden was to be closed,' John recalls. 'We didn't close it, but we spent about ten years discussing what to do next.' The development of the terrace garden has been a slow and gentle process. 'We do something,' John says, 'and then wait two or three years before doing anything else.'

Work began at the top of the site, where there was once a Victorian conservatory. They had no desire to rebuild it, but the shape and height that it gave have been re-created from wooden trellis. The footings of the original building now enclose a small, sun-soaked courtyard garden, where John has planted scented herbs. The trellis forms a shady, grotto-like space against the back wall. Inside, they have made a tufa mound that oozes water. When John and Lord Anglesey resumed work on the terraces, they focused on the second level. This was Lord Anglesey's 'philosophers' walk', and he wanted a simple, meditative space,

and this was achieved by filling the beds against the retaining wall with shrubs and plants chosen for the scent and texture of their leaves. The atmosphere on the third terrace is entirely different. Originally the beds against the retaining wall were planted with shrubs and herbaceous plants that had white or yellow flowers, and roses grew on the opposite side of the lawn. John has replaced this scheme with something bolder, wilder and altogether hotter than before. The main beds reverberate with red, gold and bronze flowers and foliage from early spring until the end of the season in October. 'Lord Anglesey doesn't like bare soil,' John explains, and the beds are certainly action packed. In July the bronze leaves and scarlet flowers of 'Bishop of Llandaff' dahlias set the tone in a bed packed with fiery crocosmias, golden achilleas, cannas, orange marigolds, tawny day lilies (*Hemerocallis*), russet-leaved euphorbias and rust-coloured rudbeckias. On the opposite side of the narrow lawn, the roses have been replaced with a block planting of blue agapanthus, echoing the blue line of the Menai Strait. John has paid particular attention to the water on the terraces, gradually amplifying its sound. At this level it pours noisily from a panther's mask on the wall, falling into a stone rill and flowing into the stone-edged lily pond that marks the centre of the terrace. It reappears, its sound greatly amplified once again by the ingenious use of a very narrow pipe, in a wall fountain below the terraces. The latest addition is an informal, pebble-lined rill that tumbles down the wooded slope above the sea.

LEFT *Parthenocissus tricuspidata* 'Veitchii' (Boston ivy) throws an exploratory tendril around a Cretan pot decorating the steps leading up to the terrace garden.

RIGHT John Dennis, head gardener, gathered agapanthus plants from all over the garden to fill this bed on the lower terrace. The repetitive pattern of the blue agapanthus flowers and acid-green lady's mantle (*Alchemilla mollis*) seem to echo the colours of the Menai Strait and the lush landscape beyond it.

BELOW The 'hot' bed on the south-facing terrace, where John Dennis creates an unbroken succession of brilliant colours from spring until mid-autumn. Tulips, dahlias and other bulbs and corms are sunk into the ground in woven plastic baskets. After flowering the baskets are pulled out to make way for the next event.

25

clwyd

bodrhyddan hall
denbighshire

Lord Langford inherited Bodrhyddan Hall from his uncle in 1951. There is a touch of magic to any story involving the inheritance of a large house and an estate set between the mountains and the sea, but this was no fairytale. The house, which Lord Langford's grandfather had commissioned W.E. Nesfield to transform in 1875, was neglected and dilapidated. 'My uncle had let everything slide,' Lord Langford recalls. Vegetables grew in the parterre beds designed by William Andrews Nesfield in the same period, and the lawns were scythed each year for hay. The area to the north of the house, where Langford's grandparents had a 'Japanese walk of life' and a sunken garden, was an impenetrable tangle of brambles and weed trees. The transformation of Bodrhyddan by the Nesfields, father and son, had been expensive and Lord Langford also inherited architect's bills unpaid by either his grandfather or his uncle, along with the inevitable death duties. A lesser man might have considered escape, although this is no real option when a house has been in your family for over six hundred years. Instead, he has worked slowly and steadily to restore the house, garden and estate.

Today the curved hedges of Nesfield's parterres are perfectly clipped. Each year Lord Langford and his two gardeners experiment with different – but always vibrant – combinations of bedding plants. Five thousand plants are needed to fill the beds. This is too many to propagate in Bodrhyddan's small greenhouse, so they are bought in from a local nursery. Lord Langford's grandmother planted yews along the edge of the parterre, and a yew walk to the west of it. Her choice of yews over roses was based on a belief that roses were too expensive. 'It's a shame,' Lord Langford remarks: 'I could buy a lot of roses for what it costs me to pay two men to clip forty-four yews each year.' The arithmetic may have been flawed, but the effect of the perfectly clipped yew is very pleasing.

The area to the north of the house is known as the Pleasance. At the top of it, close to the house and the drive, is St Mary's Well. This is said to be one of the sacred springs of Wales, and it never fails or freezes. It was probably this sure supply of water that prompted the Conwy family, Lord Langford's ancestors, to settle at Bodrhyddan. The water, which is icy and clear, runs into a seventeenth-century bathing pool. Lord Langford has never made use of this facility, although he remembers his sister immersing herself – 'but she got out pretty quickly,' he says.

Work on the Pleasance began in 1981. The site was entirely overgrown, although the remains of a path and a box hedge were discovered beneath the brambles. It is here that Lord Langford and his wife have made their mark on the garden. The neglected trees have been thinned and pruned to create a beautiful grove that rises from velvet lawns. In spring, snowdrops and daffodils flower among the trees, followed by camellias and magnolias. Ponds have been excavated in the boggy ground, their banks planted with astilbes, hostas, irises and gunneras. The latest addition to this happy scene is a summerhouse built on the summit of the mound made by Lord Langford's grandparents. Lady Langford had made a new rockery and water garden on the side of it. 'We can sit here and look at all this,' Lord Langford says, 'and feel pleased with ourselves. It's all right to feel pleased when it's just the two of you.'

BELOW The Langfords' summer house is built on a mound originally made by Lord Langford's grandparents. It has been transformed, however, by Lady Langford's new rockery and waterfall.

BELOW Lord Langford's new orangery overlooks parterres designed by W.E. Nesfield for his grandfather. The storks supporting the fountain in the foreground are part of the family crest. It can take up to a fortnight each August to clip the forty-four yews in this part of the garden.

29

chirk castle
denbighshire

Determination: some gardeners have it in such quantity that death is little more than a minor interruption in the realization of their aims. One such gardener was Lady Margaret Myddelton, who gardened at Chirk Castle from 1946 until she died in 2003. When the property was handed to the National Trust in 1981, she continued her work alongside David Lock, the Trust's head gardener. Her presence is alive today in the garden, and when you visit it David Lock will still point out areas that Lady Margaret designed and particular plant combinations that she favoured. He also recalls her habit of arriving just in time to shift the canes and string that he uses to mark out a new flowerbed, subtly altering its outline – 'and she was usually right', he observes. The Trust made no period restrictions on the planting and Lady Margaret's eclectic taste, painter's eye and love of informality still determine the atmosphere of the garden today.

Chirk is a sumptuous experience for plant lovers at any time of the year. The castle, which rises stark and impressive from the park on your approach, shows a different face to the garden. Here its ancient walls have proved perfect for growing honeysuckles such as *Lonicera tragophylla*, with its huge, yellow flowers, and the scarlet-flowered *L.* x *brownii*, which grow alongside climbing hydrangeas, roses, clematis and jasmine. The battlements and drum-shaped bastions of the building are echoed by a spectacular avenue of clipped yews and a crenellated yew hedge, all planted at the end of the nineteenth century, their perfectly modulated forms separated by terraced sweeps of velvet grass, creating a wonderfully generous and powerful impression.

Beyond the formal terraces and topiary the garden relaxes into the areas where Lady Margaret's influence is most evident. When she and Colonel Ririd Myddelton came to Chirk, they found the garden sadly neglected. Gradually they restored and remodelled every part of it. The site had been gardened since 1595, when Sir Thomas Myddelton bought the castle, a thirteenth-century fortress built to defend the border between England and Wales. Sir Thomas was a merchant venturer who invested in the voyages of Drake, Frobisher, Hawkins and Raleigh. His magnificent garden at

Chirk may have been financed by Frobisher's voyage in 1592 and the capture of a Portuguese carrack carrying cargo worth £150,000. Nothing remains of it, but Sir Thomas' account books record bills for gooseberries, a fig, vines, quinces and currants, for mowing the bowling alley and for ten weathercocks to adorn the summerhouses.

The only visible remnant of Sir Thomas' formal garden is a magnificent lime avenue that frames the view from the castle. The rest of the garden was remodelled by William Emes, a landscape architect from Derbyshire who worked in much the same style as Lancelot 'Capability' Brown. Of his seven commissions in Wales, Chirk was the largest, and took him twenty-four years to complete. He began work in 1761, replanting the park with numerous trees and excising formality from the garden. Some of Emes's beeches and oaks still grow in the park, which is divided from the garden by a ha-ha. A long, grass terrace lined with a niched yew hedge runs along the perimeter of the garden. At its far end Emes built his 'retreat seat', a small pavilion with a fine view over the park and the border counties beyond.

When Lady Margaret arrived at Chirk the area between the castle terraces and the ha-ha was occupied by herbaceous borders designed by Lady Howard de Walden, who had leased the castle with her husband from 1911 to 1946. Wartime neglect had reduced the borders to chaos. Lady Margaret redesigned the beds, creating a scalloped edge and planting them up with shrubs punctuated by stands of the flowering cherry *Prunus* 'Kanzan'. Since her death the design has been revised once again. The cherries had to be thinned out, and the planting has been made more herbaceous.

Lady Margaret's influence is at its most powerful in the Shrub Garden, where the beds, designed by Norah Lindsay for Lady Howard de Walden, had become overgrown during the war and a monumental cedar had fallen across the site. Lady Margaret's spectacular collection of flowering trees and shrubs bears a rich cargo of associations, as many of the plants were donated by close friends and family.

RIGHT, ABOVE Chirk Castle's austere and impressive façade reminds us that it was originally built for defence.

RIGHT, BELOW When the celebrated garden designer Norah Lindsay visited Chirk in the 1920s, she suggested that the yews beside the castle should be allowed to grow bigger. The gardeners heeded her advice, and these wonderful forms are the result. They are clipped once a year.

RIGHT Chirk's yew hedges have been clipped into shapes that mimic the towers and walls of the castle itself. The topiary and hedges are pruned between August and October, a process that results in two tons of yew clippings.

LEFT William Emes' 'retreat seat' overlooks the park that he remodelled. Some of the oaks that Emes planted still survive in the park today. A twenty-five year plan has been drawn up for the park, and fifty new trees are planted annually.

BELOW This building at the end of the main lawn was originally an orangery, designed by Joseph Turner. In 1912, Lord Howard de Walden converted it into a thatched aviary for his hawks.

erddig
denbighshire

According to Glynn Smith, head gardener, Erddig Hall's garden is made up of 'multiple layers'. This delightfully complex structure is the result of the largest garden restoration ever undertaken by the National Trust. Between 1975 and 1977 the Trust rescued the garden from dereliction, working to restore, re-create or visually acknowledge every phase of its development, from the original eighteenth-century layout to the final Edwardian additions.

The first layer of the garden was laid down in the late seventeenth century by Joshua Edisbury, an appealing character whose profligate spending on Erddig and generosity to family and friends reduced him to bankruptcy. John Meller, a London barrister, bought the property in 1716, and soon demolished Edisbury's small walled garden. However, its memory has been ingeniously preserved by rows of pleached limes planted by the Trust on the line of the original walls. Meller extended the house and greatly expanded the walled garden. The new walls enclosed a formal canal, broad gravel walks, summerhouses, wide lawns, scalloped yew hedges, orchards and a bowling green, a layout immortalized in a minutely detailed engraving made by Thomas Badeslade in 1740. Meller also made an inventory of all the fruit trees in the garden, a list including apricots, plums, pears, peaches and vines. These old varieties have been replanted against the long south wall. The magnificent orchards that flank the garden's main axis have also been re-created using 180 different kinds of apple, made up of a mixture of modern and eighteenth- or nineteenth-century varieties. Rows of yew pyramids add a touch of formality to the orchards and serve to flank the vista back towards the house.

The survival of Erddig's garden is due in part to the extraordinarily conservative nature of the Yorke family, squires of Erddig for over three hundred years. It seemed that heirs to the property were all christened either Philip or Simon. Simon Yorke I inherited the house from his uncle, John Meller. He continued to plant woodland on the estate, but made no changes in the garden. His son Philip Yorke I employed William Emes to beautify the park, but forbade him to touch the garden. Nothing changed until the mid-nineteenth century, when Simon Yorke III installed stalagmite fountains immediately outside the house and made a

small garden from swags of 'Dorothy Perkins' roses and pillar-grown *Clematis* 'Jackmanii' on the south side of the garden. The broad gravel walk between the rose garden and Meller's original summerhouse was then lined with formally clipped Irish yews. Towards the end of the century the planting in the garden was overlaid with rhododendrons and other Victorian shrubs, and a moss garden was made in the deep shade of the wood to the south of the canal. The final embellishment to the garden was made in 1914 by Philip Yorke II, who added Dutch gables to the pavilions on either side of the house.

Erddig reached its zenith at the beginning of the twentieth century, but the First World War stripped it of staff and the gardens gradually descended into dereliction. A visitor in the 1960s recalls being shown round by Philip Yorke III, then living in two rooms of the crumbling house. With a gesture across the overgrown garden he said, 'I think there is a pond or something out there.' He was referring, of course, to Meller's canal. By handing the property over to the National Trust, he saved it from certain destruction.

BELOW The grass beside the lake used to be mown regularly. Now that it is allowed to grow, tiny Welsh daffodils have started to flower each spring, and common orchids are found in summer.

RIGHT Orchards were already recorded on the garden plan of 1737. Before replanting, the National Trust consulted the Henry Doubleday Research Association. The result is this new orchard, still in its infancy, made up of 180 different varieties of apple that are organically managed.

BELOW The view down the canal towards the house. The path beyond the water is flanked by Portugal laurels in Versailles planting boxes.

BELOW Pyramids cut from yew
frame views of the house and
add formality to the rows of
apple trees in the walled garden.

bodnant garden

conwy

When Henry Pochin bought the Bodnant estate in 1874, he acquired a simple Georgian house with long views over the lush valley of the River Conwy and the rugged mountain landscape beyond. Pochin, who had made his fortune as an industrial chemist in Manchester, laid out the bones of a garden that was then nurtured and developed by four generations of the Aberconway family. In their hands Bodnant developed into a place of extraordinary beauty and exceptional botanical interest, an unmissable garden that encapsulates the very best in early twentieth-century planting and design.

Bodnant's garden falls into two very different areas. The house sits above a series of formal lawns and terraces. Further away, in the steep dell far below, formality gives way to naturalistic planting on a vast and ambitious scale. The two areas are deliberately isolated from each other, and the contrast between them is complete.

Pochin's house has an unlovable face, but the terraces on its west side are truly beautiful. They were designed and built between 1904 and 1914 by Henry McLaren, later the secnd Baron Aberconway, the son of Pochin's daughter Laura and her husband, Charles McLaren, the first Lord Aberconway. The first of these five terraces is known as the Upper Rose Garden, and several stone-lined rose beds punctuate its paved surface. The stone soaks up the sun and radiates warmth, coaxing the roses trained against the retaining wall to burst into flower by mid-May, and easing the existence of two centenarian *Arbutus* x *andrachnoides*, with fascinating, sculpted forms and red, papery bark. Each flowerbed is tightly packed with roses of a single variety: pink *Rosa* 'The Mayflower', white *R*. 'Margaret Merrill' and the orange *R*. 'Ann Aberconway'. Tiny, self-seeded campanulas and pools of pale saxifrage undermine any attempt at real formality in this perfumed, sun-soaked garden room, with its dramatic mountain view.

Broad stone steps link the Rose Terrace to the Croquet Terrace, named for its long and perfectly smooth lawn. The craggy stems of white *Wisteria floribunda* grip the stonework, its huge flowers filling the air with another layer of scent. At the base of the steps there is an enchanting *Wisteria venusta*, its downy, viridian leaves

BELOW LEFT A white Japanese wisteria (*W. floribunda* 'Alba') clothes the steps and the retaining wall below the Rose Terrace.

BELOW RIGHT In the Dell, the trunks of conifers rise from velvet lawns kept so clean of fallen twigs, leaves or other debris that they are reminiscent of a Japanese garden.

and long white racemes trailing in the water of a deep pool. The beds beneath the curved retaining wall of the upper terrace are packed with shrubs. Pieris grows to the height of the wall, its new leaves adding an ochre tint to beds that are already glowing with the flowers of tree peonies and of magnificent *Viburnum plicatum* and *V. macrocephalum* in spring.

Two broad staircases lead down to the Lily Terrace, their generous proportions highlighted by the great width of the coping stones on the walls that flank them. The water takes the direct route from the Croquet Terrace, falling vertically into the basin below. From the basin it is carried in a stone channel to the pool that gives this terrace its name. Pink, white, red and yellow water lilies cover its surface from midsummer until autumn sets in. Massive balustrades, infested by tiny ferns, punctuate the retaining wall of the upper terrace. The sheltered beds between them are home to an illustrious family of tender and interesting plants. Many of the specimens that originally lived here were grown from the seeds obtained by Henry McLaren from plant hunters such as Ernest Wilson, Joseph Rock, George Forrest and Frank Ludlow, making these beds an exhibition space for a magnificent collection of botanical curiosities. Today there are specimens of *Magnolia stellata* and *M. delavayii*, and a *M. grandiflora* x *virginiana* has been trained to grow flat against the wall, as has a tender *Rhododendron* 'Fragrantissimum', with its beautiful clusters of funnel-shaped white flowers, and sweetly scented *Eucryphia lucida* and *E. cordifolia*. In August, hydrangeas fill the beds with a profusion of blue and pink flowers.

The pergola and the Lower Rose Terrace are reached by handsome steps that follow the curve of the retaining wall. The wall is studded with the golden flowers of *Rosa* 'Gardenia', which fills the warm air with its rich perfume. At its upper level, a two-tiered wooden pergola is lined with 'White Triumphator' tulips in spring. The fleshy, cerise, lanterns of *Crinodendron hookerianum* swathe the walls and informal clumps of the New Zealand satin flower (*Libertia grandiflora*) colonize the lower pergola.

The Canal Terrace takes its name from the rectangular sheet of water that runs down its centre. The terrace's northern end is occupied by a green theatre planted in yew. At its southern end the view is stopped by Pin Mill, a beautiful, pale, stuccoed building that was salvaged and rebuilt in the garden by Henry McLaren. Pin Mill marks the division between the two parts of the garden, the portal to an atmosphere so absolutely different that it seems to belong to another world.

A narrow path ducks down behind the mill and leads between towering camellias, their glossy forms studded with flowers in early spring. Suddenly the air is laden with damp, mossy smells and the sound of running water. Progress is complicated by a choice of steep narrow paths, all of them leading down towards the glittering silver ribbon of the Hiraethlyn, a narrow, fast-flowing river that rushes along the floor of the Dell. The most dramatic descent can be made through an area known as the Big Rockery. Here the path follows the course of a stream as it hurries between moss-covered rocks on the steep, rocky side of the Dell. Its progress has been impeded to create small, naturalistic pools that are densely planted with a lush and beautiful combination of ferns (*Osmunda regalis*), bold, pink candelabra primulas (*P. pulverulenta*) and vivid irises.

The sheer scale of the Dell is overwhelming. Its steep sides are planted with towering banks of rhododendrons, azaleas and magnolias, and in spring it is transformed into a vertical palette splashed with astonishingly vivid swathes of colour on either side of the river. The riverbanks, which Henry Pochin stabilized, have been colonized by ferns, astilbes, hostas and blue hydrangeas. Pochin also planted an interesting collection of conifers. Among them are magnificent Japanese cedars (*Cryptomeria japonica*), Atlantic cedars (*Cedrus atlantica*) and Douglas firs (*Pseudotsuga menziesii*). Now well over a hundred years old, many of them have reached really colossal heights. At least two specimens of dawn redwood (*Metasequoia glyptostroboides*) grow near the water. This mysterious tree was thought to survive only in fossilized form until it was rediscovered in China in 1941. Watch this space, because nobody knows how tall the trees will become in maturity.

LEFT, ABOVE The climbing rose *R*. 'Gardenia' covers the wall beside the steps that lead down to the Pergola. It flowers at nose height, its powerfully sweet scent compounded by the warmth of the stone

LEFT, BELOW One of Bodnant's most famous features is this laburnum tunnel, which flowers in late May.

BELOW LEFT The delicate flowers, downy leaves and impressive woody stems of the *Wisteria venusta* which grows beside the pool at the bottom of the steps leading down from the Upper Rose Terrace to the Croquet Terrace.

BELOW RIGHT In early summer candelabra primulas, viridian moss and ferns line the edges of the stream that cascades through the Big Rockery.

powys

llowes court
brecknockshire

'We swapped our Bristol pilot cutter for this place,' says Susan Briggs. In any other context one might query the idea of exchanging a boat for a beautiful sixteenth-century house, but here in the garden of Llowes Court, anything seems possible. Susan has spent over a decade working with Roger Capps, her predecessor at Llowes, to create some of the strange magic more often associated with a Renaissance garden. I envy the first-time visitor who follows the narrow path past the pond and stumbles across one of Britain's finest and most original grottoes. 'Roger had always wanted to make a grotto,' Susan told me, 'so I told him to get on with it' – and this despite that fact that the garden was no longer his own. The result is a narrow, rock-bound space where water trickles down walls that are clothed in a continuous and fantastically patterned fabric of shells. The grotto admits little natural light, and Susan puts candles on ledges in the walls. Broken shells crunch underfoot, as though some strange and monstrous inhabitant had recently finished feasting. The grotto is just one of a series of wonderfully conceived and beautifully executed surprises in the garden.

'The land has dictated everything we have done,' Susan insists, but only in her rich and singular imagination would this close-knit tie produce such fabulous results. Take the poplar grove, for example. The trees were planted as a crop many years ago. The bottom fell out of the poplar wood market and the grove remained, its towering trunks screening long views from the house towards the Brecon Beacons. The grove has always been prone to flooding, and at some time a ditch had been dug to ease the problem. Susan noticed the winter sun illuminating the water in the ditch and this caught her imagination. She decided to build on the effect by excavating channels between the trees. Thus on a sunny winter morning shining, watery lines quarter the ground between the trunks. Susan used the excavated soil to make a mound, a soft, rounded shape that sits snugly between the vertical lines of the trees. 'The garden is always presenting us with amusements,' she remarks: 'when children jump about on the mound, it looks as though they are bouncing on the hedge behind.' Whatever next? Llowes Court may be imbued with the atmosphere of mystery and expectation that characterized the Renaissance garden, but

Susan Briggs is no Renaissance gardener. In the sixteenth century 'art' worked hard to suppress 'nature', but Susan has a much lighter touch. 'I've had years of preparing for nature,' she says, 'and then clearing up after it.' She looks around at the garden burgeoning under early-summer sun. 'You've got to make it easy for this abundance to happen,' she explains, 'but during the first week in June you must rein it in, because it atrophies.' Plants thrive under this gentle discipline. Experience has taught Susan to garden only with those that thrive naturally on the site – the ones 'whose faces fit'. The result is a great sense of wellbeing.

LEFT Leeks are left to reveal their full glory at Llowes Court, where they grow, flower and go to seed in their own sweet time.

RIGHT The narrow trunks of the poplars, pencil straight, frame a mound made out of earth excavated from drainage channels between the trees. The view beyond is towards the Brecon Beacons.

LEFT Susan Briggs was inspired by a visit to Hadspen to create this 'horse pond' at the centre of the garden. *Rosa* 'Ayrshire Splendour' cascades down the wall above the pond.

LEFT, ABOVE Roger Capps' new Mineral Tower, seen between the trees, is built into the corner of the Walled Garden. Its ceiling is encrusted with a complex pattern of semi-precious stones. Both the Mineral Tower and the inside of the Grotto were decorated by Cassie Rendle.

LEFT, BELOW Early-morning sunshine dries the washing hanging in the cobbled yard behind the house.

RIGHT, ABOVE Susan allows the herbaceous planting to run riot before she reins it in during the first week in June. There comes a point where it has to be controlled because, as she says, 'it's not a farm, it's a garden.'

RIGHT, BELOW *Rosa* 'Blairi Number 2', a vigorous Bourbon rose with fragrant semi-double flowers, thrives against the wall of the barn.

powis castle
montgomeryshire

At the end of the seventeenth century the Marquess of Powis decided to transform the steep, rugged slope beneath the castle into a garden. Plans were commissioned from William Winde, architect of the gardens at Cliveden in Buckinghamshire, and three long terraces were blasted out of the rock on which the castle is built. Winde's elegant terraces have remained virtually unchanged, making Powis one of very few Italianate Baroque gardens to have survived intact in Britain.

The garden was expanded at the beginning of the seventeenth century, when a flamboyant Dutch water garden was laid out on level ground at the base of the slope, the area now known as the Great Lawn. The late 1770s saw William Emes called in to work his magic on the park. Emes was a devotee of 'Capability' Brown's naturalistic style, and he advised the 1st Earl of Powis to dismantle Winde's contrived terraces and smooth the ground into a grassy slope. The Earl rejected this suggestion, but permitted Emes to fill in the pools and fountains of the water garden and to transform the ridge opposite the castle into a beautiful wilderness composed of decorative trees and narrow, winding paths.

By the end of the century the terraces were under threat again, this time from neglect. Steps and balustrades had begun to crumble and give way and horses were reported grazing the parterres. The rigorous pruning regime applied to the yew hedges and obelisks planted on the terraces had become relaxed. For a while they grew freely, but the nineteenth century saw an attempt to control their growth more tightly once again. Peter Hall, head gardener, describes the management of the Powis yews as a series of 'happy mistakes' – mistakes that transformed their tight, geometric forms into the wonderfully generous, overblown and amorphous shapes that dominate the garden today.

The next important moment for Powis came at the beginning of the twentieth century when Violet, Countess of Powis and wife to the 4th Earl, took over the management of the garden. It was her ambition to propel Powis out of mediocrity and make the garden into 'one of the most beautiful, if not the most beautiful, in England and Wales'. Mission accomplished. Powis can most certainly lay claim to the title to which the Countess aspired, and it could probably carry off an additional award as one of Britain's most theatrical gardens. The site is dramatic, and so is the looming presence of the castle, but the real drama is played out between the formality of Winde's design and the louche, undisciplined yew trees and hedges that threaten to collapse, like dough left too long to rise, over the edges of the terraces.

The entrance to the garden today is from the western end of the top terrace, where the clipped yew trees make their presence felt immediately by capriciously screening and then revealing a long and magnificent view across the Border landscape. The beds on this terrace are devoted to 'tropical effect' planting. Most of the plants that the gardeners pack into them in early summer will have been over-wintered or propagated in the glasshouses. Powis is fortunate to have retained its glasshouses and Peter Hall believes that they have an important impact on the character of the whole garden, and in particular of this top terrace. 'If you can propagate your own plants,' he explains, 'you can experiment without risking a lot of money.' He believes that this encourages a 'trial mentality' at Powis, and a tendency towards 'flamboyant and innovative' planting. By July the plants in the warm, south-facing beds have bulked up, and the intense blue flowers of *Salvia* 'Indigo Spires' rub shoulders with ochre and yellow abutilons, pink fuchsias, the bronze leaves of *Musa coccinea* and the red flowers of *Cestrum elegans*, creating an impression that Peter is right to describe as 'full and lush'. He admits that everyone has the opportunity to buy striking, tender plants these days, but at Powis they always aim to include a few 'surprises' among the planting each year. At the end of the season the beds are stripped down and many of the larger plants are discarded. Between November and May the beds lie virtually empty, and the gardeners take this opportunity to thoroughly clean and enrich the soil.

Lead shepherds and shepherdesses made by John van Nost in the seventeenth century do a perpetual dance across the balustrade of the second terrace, which takes its name from the aviary built against its retaining wall. The eastern end of the building is draped in a cascade of *Wisteria floribunda* and yellow *Rosa banksiae* 'Lutea'. Instead of birds the aviary shelters a *Ficus pumila* that papers the ceiling with its tiny leaves, and wonderfully decorative chain ferns (*Woodwardia radicans*). Outside, a narrow,

RIGHT, ABOVE Seventeenth-century urns and statues decorate the balustrade of the Aviary Terrace. They were all produced in the workshop of Flemish sculptor John van Nost. The statues are made from lead, and in the eighteenth century would have been painted to imitate marble or other expensive materials. Today they have a coating that resembles weathered lead.

RIGHT, BELOW The Orangery Terrace is at the bottom of this picture, with the Aviary Terrace and the Top Terrace piled on top of it like the layers of a wedding cake. The amorphous yews seem ready to cascade, like melting icing, over the terraces below them.

ABOVE The hedges are a distinctive and engaging feature of the garden. They were originally planted *c.*1680 and since then they have been maintained in a variety of different ways. Today pruning begins in August and is done with electric hedge trimmers. It takes four members of staff three months to complete the job.

RIGHT A statue of Hercules by John van Nost, at the eastern end of the Top Terrace.

sun-baked bed lines the retaining wall. It is a heaven for cistuses
of all varieties, and for irises, whose gnarled corms bask in the
heat. Climbing roses such as *R*. 'Gloire de Dijon' and *R*. 'Madame
Caroline Testout' scramble up the wall behind them.

Powis's top terrace is slightly tropical, and its second slightly
Mediterranean, but the double herbaceous borders on the
Orangery Terrace are entirely British. Clematis scrambles over
metal domes, as it has ever since the nineteenth century, and in
early summer peonies, poppies and irises steal the show. The
orangery still shelters a few cistus trees each winter, and in
summer they stand on the terrace outside. Beyond them the
terrace disappears into the belly of the great yew hedge that
tumbles down the hill at its far end. The path beyond it is a narrow
channel between towering walls of venerable box.

In 1912, shortly after Violet, Countess of Powis, took over the
garden, a storm felled several large elms. Their absence exposed
a view over the kitchen garden and greenhouses that Violet
considered 'detestable'. Her solution was to transform the level
space into an extension of the ornamental garden, planting it with
a mixture of flowers and fruit trees that might be found in any
Edwardian cottage garden, although here the scale is
monumental. In the Fountain Garden beyond, the Countess's
style became more formal. Clipped box lines an ample lawn with
a fountain at its centre.

Emes's Wilderness occupies a ridge overlooking the vast,
velvety expanse of the Great Lawn. It is a romantic place, equally
suited to lovers' trysts and solitary wandering. Emes's planting
was greatly enriched in the nineteenth century, when sessile oaks,
Japanese cedars (*Cryptomeria japonica*), tulip trees (*Liriodendron
tulipifera*), wellingtonias and many other interesting specimens
were introduced. The stony ridge is swathed in acid soil, creating
ideal conditions for the rhododendrons and azaleas that line the
twisting paths. In spring the air is heavy with the sweet scent of
the lovely, deciduous azalea *Rhododendron luteum*.

FAR LEFT, ABOVE John van Nost's light-hearted lead figures are to be found all over the garden.

LEFT, ABOVE This statue was inspired by the marble Venus de' Medici that is now in Florence's Uffizi Gallery. It stands at the western end of the Orangery Terrace.

LEFT, BELOW Cistus grows happily against the warm wall of the Aviary Terrace.

RIGHT The view from the Fountain Garden towards the red-sandstone bulk of the castle. From this perspective it is possible to appreciate the varied planting of the different terraces. The informal Apple Slope can just be seen below the Orangery Terrace. It is spectacular in autumn, when the leaves of the Japanese maples and amelanchiers planted there turn orange and scarlet,

dyfed

aberglasney
carmarthenshire

If this were a fairytale, Aberglasney would be its heroine. A garden orphaned and abandoned, its walls crumbling beneath the weight of ivy, was rescued from dereliction and restored to great beauty by a princely gathering of well-wishers and a combination of private and public funding. The tale has a happy ending and today Aberglasney is a vibrant, successful place. The garden is as precious for the fragments of its Jacobean layout as for the rich and imaginative contemporary planting that spills out of the original walled enclosures and into the woods above and below the house. This successful combination reflects the attitude of Graham Rankin, Aberglasney's director, who has been determined to create horticultural interest throughout the year. 'The garden is almost more beautiful in winter than summer,' he says. 'We leave a lot of the herbaceous plants standing, and on a frosty morning there is nothing more lovely than their seed heads.'

On a fine August day it's hard to believe that anything could be lovelier than Aberglasney in midsummer. The Jacobean cloister that stands below the west façade of the house was the garden's ticket to redemption, a unique and fascinating relic that could not be allowed to disappear. The cloister, a wonderful structure that oozes stalactites, occupies only one side of the enclosure. It is flanked by two walls punctuated by blind arches. Steps lead up to a broad walkway that runs along the top of the walls, giving a first glimpse of the extraordinary variety of pleasures that the garden has in store. There are no records to show how Bishop Rudd, who built the garden in about 1600, originally planted the area enclosed by the walls. The grass parterre, spiked by tulips and hyacinths in spring, is copied from an early seventeenth-century painting. In summer it is furnished with handsome pots of citrus, their presence justified by records of oranges grown at St Donat's in Glamorgan at the end of the sixteenth century. When winter comes and the citrus trees

retreat to the glasshouse, weighty balls of box take their place.

The pared-down simplicity of the cloister continues in the next enclosure, which is entirely occupied by a rectangular, stone-lined pool. The large space is filled by the sound of the spring water that pours into the pool from steep, stone channels ranged along its edges. Aberglasney gives great pleasure, and part of that pleasure derives from an extraordinarily high level of maintenance. Weed is dredged from the pool each morning in summer, and the water pouring down the channels is clear and sweet.

The garden is rich in water, some of it off the hills and some from springs that rise in the garden itself. The plants in the two walled gardens appear to thrive on a diet of abundant water and manure, an impression that Graham Rankin confirms. 'This year,' he says, 'we brought in a weight of manure equivalent to six double-decker buses.' The walled gardens were originally used to grow fruit, cutting flowers and vegetables. Today the smaller of the two enclosures combines all these functions to great and highly ornamental effect. The upper garden was laid out in 1999 by Penelope Hobhouse, garden designer, historian and author. A fine mixture of old and modern perennials, shrubs and climbers thrive in oval, box-lined beds that tilt engagingly towards the view.

Aberglasney attracts 50,000 visitors each year and thus, uniquely, it is able to cover its operational costs from ticket sales alone. Part of its success must be due to the continuing development of the garden. Take the scruffy little wood above the house. Four years ago it contained nothing but ash saplings, undergrowth and a narrow stream. Now it is the site of the Oriental Garden, a wonderful collection of peonies, meconopsis, magnolias and camellias that have been planted in the dappled shade over the past four years. The stream runs on, packed with candelabra primulas and ferns.

ABOVE LEFT A view towards the house across the beds of the Upper Walled Garden, where the layout was designed by Penelope Hobhouse.

LEFT In summer, oranges in lead planters are set out in the Cloister Garden. The containers are purpose-made, and each one is inscribed with the letter 'A'. In winter, the oranges are replaced with balls of clipped box.

BELOW Summer in the Cloister Garden, with lavender and oranges seen from inside the arched enclosure. In the seventeenth century the Cloister Garden's grass parterre would have been 'enamelled' with scented bulbs. Today, tulips are used to re-create this effect each spring.

BELOW An elegant wooden bridge crosses the stream running through the woods above the house. A network of inviting paths has been made to lead visitors through the woods, where a wonderful new collection of plants is beginning to thrive in the dappled shade.

BOTTOM Candelabra primulas and ferns line the stream in the wood above the house.

BELOW The Upper Walled Garden was originally used to grow fruit and vegetables, but after years of neglect it was derelict. The tilting, box-lined beds on the site today were designed by Penelope Hobhouse and planted in 1999.

ON PAGES 66–7 The Pool Garden, seen through the branches of a weeping ash. The pool was probably originally used to raise fish for the kitchen, but now it is a highly ornamental feature of the garden.

national botanic garden of wales
carmarthenshire

It wasn't a fair question to put to someone midway through a day of intensive tree planting, but I put it nevertheless. 'What would you say were the aims of the National Botanic Garden of Wales?' I asked. The answer came swiftly and with a smile: 'Education, conservation and the creation of a world-class botanic garden.' Eight years after the garden opened in May 2000, there can be no doubt that the National Botanic Garden is triumphantly realizing these ambitions. It is also fulfilling another, unspoken remit: the duty to entertain – in all weathers. On cold or wet days the Double Walled Garden, the woods and the lake may lose their charm, but visitors are still drawn by Norman Foster's magnificent Great Glass House and the Tropical House that opened in 2007 to display a riveting and dramatic collection of gingers, palms, aroids, orchids and bromeliads. It's just bad luck if your visit happens to coincide with the flowering of the *Amorphophallus konjac*, when the Tropical House is filled with a smell that one gardener defines as being 'somewhere between rotting meat and old urine'.

The Great Glass House sits comfortably in the landscape, its gently domed roof scarcely interrupting the continuity of the rolling hills around the garden. The building breaks records: its elliptical dome measures 272 x 158 feet/95 x 55 metres, and this makes it the biggest single-span glass building in the world. It is designed to create the ideal conditions for Mediterranean-climate plants from both the northern and southern hemispheres. To this end the dome is tilted towards the south to catch maximum sunlight, and a concrete wall to the north shields the interior from the coldest winds. This design means that the interior requires minimal heating, and even on the dullest day it is bathed in light. The interior temperature is carefully controlled by glass panels that pivot up and down automatically to create an ideal airflow. A

RIGHT Norman Foster's Great Glass House shelters a landscape designed by Kathryn Gustafson and planted with Mediterranean-climate flora from all over the world. Although regions with a Mediterranean climate cover less than 2 per cent of the Earth's surface, they contain more than 20 per cent of all known flowering plant species.

LEFT The Tropical House, designed by John Belle, is seen here across the Double Walled Garden. Most of the plants inside it are monocots (plants that emerge from the ground with one seed leaf). Many belong to five of the most important tropical plant families – the orchids, gingers, aroids, palms and bromeliads.

LEFT, ABOVE An azalea flowers among ferns above the lake.

LEFT, BELOW In Paxton's day the Walled Garden was used to produce fruit and vegetables for the family. Today it is divided into four quadrants that have been filled with plants carefully selected and arranged to illustrate the evolution of flowering plants. Only the fourth quadrant is used for food production.

ABOVE The conditions inside the Great Glass House are kept as natural as possible, with light, shade, irrigation and temperature being carefully adjusted to meet the needs of a huge variety of plants. Outside, silver birch (*Betula utilis* var. *jacquemontii*) lines the path.

ON PAGES 72–3 The Great Glass House sits quite comfortably in its rural surroundings. The building next to it is Principality House, the only part of Paxton's original mansion to have survived. It was built to house the servants' quarters, brew house, laundry and kitchens. The main house was destroyed by fire in 1931.

biomass boiler provides background heat here and in the offices and shops. By 2010 the estate's own plantations of miscanthus, willow and poplar will be mature enough for coppicing, making the Botanic Garden self-sufficient in fuel.

Norman Foster's great glass dome shelters plants from central Chile, California, the Canary Islands, south-west Australia, South Africa's Cape and Europe's Mediterranean Basin. In the wild their existence might be threatened by population growth, tourism, drought, agricultural and industrial expansion or even fire. Here, they thrive in the safety of a protected and perfected landscape that was deigned by Kathryn Gustafson and described in the New York Times as 'a Grand Canyon under a glass sky'. It is an extraordinarily dramatic combination of cliffs, rocky terraces, gullies, streams, waterfalls and plateaux that are cleverly strung together by narrow paths and bridges. Plants and trees have rapidly smothered the hard landscaping, so that now the effect is highly naturalistic. Each season brings its own entertainments. In early summer the immense, waxy-pink flowers of proteas dominate the South African zone, while Australia glows with the intensely coloured, curiously furry buds of the kangaroo paw (*Anigozanthos manglesii*), and *Geranium maderense*, with its huge, spider-like heads, blooms in the Canaries.

The Double Walled Garden was built at the end of the eighteenth century, when William Paxton bought the Middleton estate, built a splendid, neo-classical house and surrounded it with a fabulous park enriched with lakes, streams and cascades. The double wall is a curiosity, a riddle that has not been properly solved. No one knows exactly what the architect hoped to gain by building a brick wall to surround the stone one, but we may be sure that he was operating at the cutting edge of contemporary theory. During Paxton's lifetime a wide range of fruit – including strawberries, pineapples, peaches and apricots – would have grown here alongside vegetables and cutting flowers for the house. Today the garden is divided into four sections. Three of them are ingeniously designed to provide a visual history of 140 million years of botanical evolution. The fourth section is given over to allotments, which are planted and maintained by the pupils and teachers of local schools. Each year the Botanic Garden offers courses in plant propagation to teachers, and in April participating schools receive a range of different seeds. They plant these after the Easter holidays, and in June staff and pupils bring their seedlings to the Double Walled Garden to plant up. Gardeners maintain the allotments over the summer, but in September the children return to harvest their crops. This experience brings new meaning to Harvest Festival back at school, and afterwards the children learn how to prepare healthy dishes from their produce.

The garden is in its infancy, and this makes it an exciting, vibrant place. There is room on the 500-acre/202-hectare estate for new ideas to be realized, and the ideas come thick and fast. Take the Woods of the World project, for example, where the woodlands of countries with a climate akin to that of Wales are being re-created. To this end trees from Chile, Tasmania, Japan, the United States and China's Yangtze Basin have been planted in yet another fascinating area of the garden.

the cilwendeg shell house
pembrokeshire

The Shell House stands in a narrow clearing in the woods beside Cilwendeg Mansion. It is a tiny, neo-Gothic cottage that was built in about 1820 from local stone and adorned with shards and pinnacles of glowing quartz. The interior is decorated with dense shellwork patterns that entirely cover the walls and the ceiling. The shells, like the building materials, are local. According to Blott Kerr-Wilson, shell artist extraordinaire, this makes the Cilwendeg Shell House extremely unusual. Blott believes that the majority of shell houses and grottoes were decorated with exotic shells brought back as gifts to the lady of the house by the captains of ships in which their husbands had invested. At Cilwendeg it is more likely that the ladies made their own shell-collecting expeditions to local beaches for, with the exception of a very few huge pink conch shells from the West Indies, all the surviving shells are indigenous to the beaches of Pembrokeshire and Cardigan Bay.

The Temple Trust, a fundraising organization devoted to the preservation of ornamental garden buildings, commissioned Blott Kerr-Wilson to restore the Shell House. It was in a semi-derelict state, but shards of mussel, cockle and limpet shells had survived, buried in the original lime mortar on the walls. Archaeologists who excavated the area around the building also recovered other shells and hundreds of fragments of coloured glass, quartz crystal and polished stones, pieces of coal and gunflints. These survivors were all re-used, but Blott's first task was to collect new shells. She spent a happy month 'dodging the tides' on beaches from Pembroke to Borth. The patterns that she made on the walls and ceilings are composed of 'the common shells that we all collected as children', with the addition of a batch of oysters sent to her by an oyster farm in Sussex. 'The oysters had gone off,' Blott recalls, 'and I had a call from the courier to say that he had a very smelly delivery for me.' Those oysters now sit among the mussels, whelks, scallops, razor and other shells, tiny crystals, coloured glass and even coal that Blott has worked into a continuous fabric over the entire surface of walls and ceiling. The end result is so lavish and extraordinary that it would be worth travelling to west Wales just to see it.

LEFT AND RIGHT The walls of the Shell House are decorated with a series of gothic arches picked out in dark mussel shells and filled with repeating patterns made from mussels, whelks, limpets and snails and the shining inside surfaces of oyster and razor shells. Mineral-clad owls gaze from the corners of the room.

Ffynone
pembrokeshire

RIGHT John Nash's original façade was rendered almost unrecognizable by F. Inigo Thomas, who remodelled it at the beginning of the twentieth century.

The young John Nash built Ffynone for the Colby family in 1793. Colonel Colby planted at least sixty thousand trees around the new house, and some survive to this day, a venerable presence nursed on by Ffynone's copious supplies of water. At the beginning of the twentieth century the current Colby, a keen big game hunter, arranged to go to Siberia to shoot bears. His wife said she would like to make a few alterations to the house in his absence. He was planning to be away for eighteen months, so perhaps it was guilt that inspired him to give her *carte blanche*. By the time he got home, F. Inigo Thomas had remodelled the exterior of the house and laid the generous terrace and the lawns on its west side. Perhaps Colby learned his lesson, for he is said to have scarcely recognized his home and, furthermore, he had an enormous bill to pay.

Earl Lloyd George has lived at Ffynone since 1987. 'When we first came here,' he told me, 'you couldn't even tell where the garden was meant to be.' He hacked his way into the woods that tumble down the hill beside the house, cutting through brambles 'as thick as a man's wrist', to reveal the original structure. Laurel and *Rhododendron ponticum* that had been allowed to grow unchecked for many years needed to be reined back, fallen timber cleared and weed trees felled. At the foot of the hill he found a Victorian fountain, its shaft in pieces and its bowl dry and choked with weeds. Weeds also grew between the slabs of the terrace in front of the house, where a huge stone urn had toppled off the wall and hung suspended in the branches of an overhanging yew. Earl Lloyd George had just retired but, he recalls, 'I had never worked so hard in my life.'

By 1988 he was ready to embark on re-planting. He had always been a gardener, like his mother before him, but he had never had

Stepping stones lead across the lily pond to a building that has always been known as the workhouse. The pool lies at one end of Inigo Thomas' new terrace behind the house. It is partially enclosed by a curved wall swathed in a 'Rambling Rector' rose.

the opportunity to work on acid soil. Ericaceous plants became a passion, and he has transformed Ffynone's woodland garden into a gallery for a huge and varied collection of rhododendrons that he has built up over the years. Today there are over six hundred plants of 120 different kinds. When the garden opens for the National Garden Scheme each spring, visitors find the woods transformed into an extraordinary, living paintbox of colours created by the great swathes of rhododendrons and azaleas in flower. The trees are underplanted with pieris, eucryphias, kalmias, camellias and a huge range of ferns.

Earl Lloyd George has restored the
Victorian fountain that he discovered
beneath the undergrowth at the
bottom of the hill.

picton castle
pembrokeshire

Picton's gardens surround a thirteenth-century castle that has belonged since the late fifteenth century to the Philipps – Pembrokeshire's most powerful family during the seventeenth and eighteenth centuries. The garden covers 40 acres/16 hectares, and encompasses a large and informal area of woodland, an important collection of unusual rhododendrons, a fernery and a nineteenth-century walled garden containing, among other things, a collection of medicinal herbs.

Towards the end of the eighteenth century Richard Philips, Lord Milford, extended the family castle, added some fashionable Georgian interiors and created a picturesque walk that wound its way through the woods towards the river. This was the beginning of the fabulous woodland garden that is Picton's most important feature. Today the woodland area is deliberately gardened with a light hand, and this allows plenty of scope for wild flowers, small animals and insects to thrive. The rich, acid soil and the mild, damp climate create perfect conditions for the rhododendrons and azaleas that grow under the ancient oaks and beeches. Many of the rhododendrons, such as R. 'Picton Palette' and R. 'Picton Adonis' are unique to the garden.

Picton's woodland garden is also home to an outstanding collection of ferns. Roddy Milne, Head Gardener, has spent the past fourteen years transforming a damp corner of the woods into a theatrical glade where tree ferns tower above a dense carpet of *Onoclea sensibilis* (the sensitive fern) interplanted with other varieties to create a series of wonderful contrasts. Elsewhere, Roddy Milne has planted other imaginative combinations of ferns among rhododendrons, bamboos and herbaceous plants. There is also a fern walk, where native and exotic ferns grow side by side, and a fernery for less hardy species.

LEFT Picton Castle seen from the south lawn. During the seventeenth and eighteenth centuries the castle was a focus for local social, political and cultural life.

LEFT Ferns thrive in the dappled shade of the trees, and they are a vital feature of the woodland garden.

BELOW Water lilies and arum lilies (*Zantedeschia aethiopica*) in the pond at the centre of the walled garden.

rhos-y-gilwen mansion
pembrokeshire

You might go to Rhos-y-Gilwen to attend a concert in the purpose-built hall, or to spend a night in the comfortable mid-Victorian house. Whatever your motive, be absolutely sure to visit the walled garden that was built at the same time as the house.

Too many of Wales' walled gardens have been abandoned to grass and weeds, and their glasshouses allowed to fall into dereliction. This was the situation at Rhos-y-Gilwen until eight years ago, when Brenda Squires and Glen Peters made the inspired decision to employ John Thomas, a local man, to restore the garden to peak condition. It was a daunting job. The walls enclosed an acre of land that had been abandoned for nearly fifty years, and the ground was infested with couch grass and brambles. Thomas did not resort to machinery or weedkiller; he simply divided the site into small plots and dug it, clearing each plot slowly and methodically. The old fig trees still thrived against the garden wall, but most of the other fruit trees had gone. Thomas made new plantings of apples, pears, plums and cherries. Today, like a Victorian head gardener, he produces all the fruit, vegetables and cut flowers for the house. He has a good eye, and he has made a wonderful, dense tapestry of the vegetables, which seem to thrive in his care.

State-of-the-art glasshouses had been erected in the walled garden at the beginning of the twentieth century. By the time Thomas started work, the subterranean boiler that powered the heating system had gone for scrap and the glasshouses were derelict. In 2003 Brenda Squires and Glen Peters decided to restore them. Enough of the original features remained for the builders to reconstruct the Edwardian design. Under Thomas' care the glasshouses rapidly came back into full production. He planted a vine outside one end of the building, feeding its stem through the original vine arch at the bottom of the wall; peaches and nectarines already fruit heavily against the wall in summer; and tomatoes grow up an ingenious grid of canes arranged to his own design.

ABOVE Peaches were recently planted against the wall in the restored glass house, and already they are heavy with fruit.

RIGHT, ABOVE A section of the walled garden is devoted to cutting flowers. In June lupins and poppies dominate the scene.

RIGHT, BELOW John Thomas, seen here weeding a row of carrots, keeps the garden in a near-perfect condition with the help of only one part-time gardener.

llanllyr
ceredigion

Llanllyr is that wonderful thing: a beautiful garden that has obviously been much fun in the making. When Loveday Gee moved back to her family home, there wasn't much of a garden at Llanllyr. 'My father just farmed,' she explains, 'and my mother said gardening gave her indigestion.' That was in 1986, and since then Loveday and her husband Robert have developed a marvellously quirky 7-acre/3-hectare garden that is the product of Loveday's desire to create 'a garden with a reason'. Beauty just isn't enough for her. In her hands a garden must work twice as hard, being beautiful, as Llanllyr most certainly is, but also giving visual expression to a number of different thoughts and ideas. The references within the garden that have become the themes of her design include fourteenth-century poetry, Italian art, the medieval history of Llanllyr, the lives of her grandchildren and important family events such as weddings and anniversaries.

Work began after Loveday went into hospital for a minor operation. When she returned home, she was greeted by one of her sons. 'I've had the bulldozer in the shrubbery,' he said, 'so now you can start planting it up.' Loveday would explain the success of Llanllyr as a series of happy accidents and coincidences, but here in the shrubbery, close to the house, her sharp eye for striking colour combinations and pleasing contrasts of texture is immediately obvious. A brilliant selection of ornamental trees, including *Cornus kousa* and a variety of maples, line the winding paths. Beneath them the ground is densely planted with ferns and geraniums.

The rose garden forms the heart of Llanllyr. It is planted on the site of a double herbaceous border created by Loveday's grandmother. Today the beds are packed with 500 roses, their scent trapped and intensified by a high, clay wall on one side and

RIGHT, ABOVE *Rosa gallica* 'Versicolor' ('Rosa Mundi'), one of the old roses that grow on the sunnier side of the walled garden.

RIGHT, BELOW Pink roses interwoven with the tiny flowers of *Allium campanulatum* create the effect of a wonderful tapestry.

BELOW In the rose garden, five
hundred roses combine with a
rich palette of other plants to
form a continuous fabric of scent
and colour.

LEFT, ABOVE The flowers of love-in-a-mist (*Nigella damascena*) push their way through the lower stems of the Gallica rose 'Tuscany Superb'.

LEFT, BELOW Primulas in a wonderful range of sherbet shades line the paths around the pond, which is the latest feature to be added to the garden.

a yew hedge on the other. The beds were planted in 1990 to a design by Hazel le Rougetel. Loveday has kept the original design in mind, but over the years she has adjusted and perfected it, moving the old roses to the sunnier side of the site and planting David Austin's modern roses in the shadier bed. She has adhered to Hazel le Rougetel's scheme for the underplanting. Thus white roses are always underplanted with acid-green foliage plants, apricot roses with bronze, pale pink with glaucous colours, dark pink with silver and crimson with blue. The result is a startling success and a vivid celebration of summer.

Beyond the roses Loveday has made her Italian garden, a narrow, stone rill lined with serpentine yew hedges. Robert would have liked to have expanded on Loveday's tribute to Italy, a country that she has known and loved for most of her life, by installing *giochi d'acqua* – water tricks that are characteristic of Italy's sixteenth- and seventeenth-century gardens – but he eventually had to concede that the Welsh climate would rob them of their humour. Instead he created a toned-down version: a series of jets that rise, unexpected but harmless, from the edges of the terrace.

Reading *Piers Plowman*, the allegorical poem written by Langland in the fourteenth century, inspired Loveday to plant a maze from escallonia hedges. She has marked the path through the maze with flowering plants. Visitors who follow the colours of the rainbow will find their way to its heart, as long as they are not distracted by multiple sins on the way. Outside the labyrinth a modern version of the Renaissance orchard, where flowering trees were 'underplanted with roses and other pleasures', has been created with radiating avenues of the crab apple *Malus* x *robusta* 'Red Sentinel' and the lovely ornamental cherry *Prunus* 'Taihaku'. On its eastern boundary there is a mount. A polished granite sculpture on the summit represents a flame that symbolizes 'the continuity of time, history and the natural world'. How typical it is in this endearing garden to find very small and rather comic statues of meercats on the mount's sloping sides. These figures, which undermine the high-minded message of the sculpture, were installed by some of the Gees' many grandchildren. They represent nothing more complex than four children who love this magical place.

cae hir gardens
ceredigion

Wil Akkermans comes from a line of Dutch nurserymen stretching back over two hundred years. His grandfather, father, uncles and now nephews have all owned tree nurseries. When Wil left his teaching job in Holland and moved to Wales, however, it was never his intention to make a garden. The inspiration came from a visit to Wisley. 'Suddenly I knew,' he remembers, 'and I said to myself, "I'm going to do something like this, on a small scale."' Twenty-five years on, Wil admits that he was 'totally mad', but he has never regretted his decision, and he sums the whole process up as 'a massive adventure'.

Cae Hir's garden covers 6 acres/2.5 hectares, intensely worked. Originally there were three steep fields behind the house and a rather boggy area on the other side of the road. Wil has transformed this site, alone and using almost nothing but hand tools, into a series of enclosures loosely linked by lawns, steps, groves and winding paths. 'I'm not a plant collector,' he explains; 'I'm more interested in the bigger picture.' He knows his plants, however, and despite side-stepping the family business, he also knows his trees. While he was still living in Holland, he saw a 'yellow' garden made during the 1930s. 'It might sound boastful,' he says, 'but I thought, I can do better than that.' At Cae Hir he has proved his point by creating Yellow, Red and Blue Gardens. He does not rely on the transient effect of flowers to create these impressions. 'Growing up in a tree nursery taught me about the different colours of foliage that are available,' he explains.

The Yellow Garden is Wil's own El Dorado. Golden conifers create a screen behind a space densely planted with golden-leaved varieties of holly, philadelphus, privet, elder and rowan. The shrubs and trees are inter-planted with yellow roses, the yellow Turk's cap lily (*Lilium pyrenaicum*), yellow and orange varieties of crocosmia, Welsh poppies (*Meconopsis cambrica*) and lady's mantle (*Alchemilla mollis*).

After this radiant space, the Red Garden seems very sombre. It is enclosed by bronze-leaved, berberis hedges that give a red cast to the light. 'I'm not too keen on it myself,' Wil admits, disarmingly. He began by using red flowers, but soon found their clashing colours intolerable. Now the beds are filled with herbaceous plants that have pink or purple flowers. Wil would be

the first to admit that it's quite a relief to get outside and feast your eyes on the fresh greens of lawns and trees.

Wil makes no real distinction between wild and cultivated plants. He often encourages wild species to invade the garden, although sometimes they turn out to be thugs and he regrets inviting them in. One of the most striking plant combinations is in a bed at the centre of the garden, where Wil has made a massed planting of wild butterbur (*Petasites hybridus*), punctuated by the lance-shaped leaves of crocosmia. He has planted several specimen trees in the garden, having propagated many of them from seed, but this does not diminish his appreciation of the original trees on the site. He is particularly fond of a pair of gnarled hawthorns that formed part of the hedge that once divided the site.

On the other side of the road Wil has created a garden around a series of ponds. The ponds were his solution to the boggy ground at the bottom of the site. Even Wil could not dig them single handed, so a JCB was hired. 'The holes filled with water as soon as they were dug,' he recalls. Twenty-five years on, the ponds look as though they have always been there, their banks packed with drifts of wild flowers and a few of Wil's artful introductions.

Next year, Wil plans to begin the process of handing the management of Cae Hir over to his son and one of his daughters. He had intended to sell up, but his children wouldn't hear of it. It's hard to imagine Wil retiring, and I don't suppose that he really intends to. He sometimes looks at the garden today and thinks, 'Every tree, every stone, every thing has passed through my hands. You couldn't say that I've been lazy.' I shouldn't think he even knows how to be lazy.

ABOVE A feature of the garden is effective combinations of wild and cultivated plants. In this bed the huge, circular leaves of butterbur (*Petasites hybridus*) are teamed with lance-shaped crocosmia leaves.

RIGHT This pond is cut into the slope about half way up the garden. The columns were made from moulded concrete.

gwent

clytha park
monmouthshire

The park at Clytha was laid out in 1790 by John Davenport for William Jones. Davenport also designed a large walled garden and a magnificent castle-shaped folly that serves as an eye-catcher on the hill to the south-west of the house. In 1820 the old house was demolished and Jones' great-nephew and heir, another William Jones, commissioned Edward Haycock, a fashionable architect from Shrewsbury, to design a new building in the Greek Revival style. Little changed in the park, but most of the ornamental canal that Davenport had made in the garden was transformed into a much more fashionable lake, and the spoil from this lake was used to raise the new house up above the flood plain. In the early twentieth century, Avray Tipping was invited to remodel parts of the garden. A line of apple trees beside the remains of Davenport's canal are known to have been planted by him. The planting of the area surrounding the lake has been progressively enriched by the Hanbury-Tenisons, who have lived at Clytha for many years.

RIGHT, ABOVE Rhododendrons, gunnera and yellow flag irises grow on the shores of the lake.

RIGHT, BELOW The fruit and vegetable garden is surrounded by the D-shaped walls that were Davenport's signature.

BELOW A broad, grassy walk leads
under the weeping willow on the
lake's west bank to a boathouse that
is painted a glorious shade of
duck-egg blue.

dewstow gardens and grottoes
monmouthshire

Everybody loves a 'forgotten' garden, a garden that has been 'hidden' or 'lost'. Dewstow can lay claim to all these titles, and even add 'buried' to the list. Stories of this kind need a happy ending and, once again, Dewstow scores high marks in this respect. Since the current owners rediscovered it in 2000, the garden has been carefully restored to its full, very surprising and eccentric glory.

The restoration has been an unusual job, because much of the garden lies in a series of subterranean grottoes linked by tunnels. This extraordinary design was the work of Henry Oakley, who bought the Dewstow estate in 1893, and of James Pulham & Son, landscape architects who specialized in the creation of rockeries, ferneries, follies and grottoes and invented a very convincing form of artificial rock made from proprietary cement modelled over wire. Pulham's 'rock builders' were trained to sculpt the surface of the cement, creating colours and textures similar to those of natural rock. Pulhamite, as it was known, became very fashionable, but nowhere else was it used on such a grand scale as at Dewstow. At ground level in the gardens, which cover nearly 7 acres/3 hectares, there were rockeries, artificial pools and waterfalls made from Pulhamite and natural stone. The walls of the subterranean grottoes between them were clad in a mixture of tufa (a porous rock formed around mineral springs) and Pulhamite.

Dewstow thrived as long as Henry Oakley was alive, but his death in 1940 marked the beginning of the garden's decline. By the end of the war cows were grazing the site, and Oakley's tropical glasshouse had been re-roofed with corrugated asbestos, given a new concrete floor and made into a barn. When the M4 motorway was built, Dewstow's owners used the spoil to fill in the grottoes, pools and rock gardens. Strangely, this treatment did not spell total destruction, but the garden was soon entirely forgotten, and this is the romance of the story. When the Harris family bought the house in 2000, they were mystified by the strange rocks protruding from the ground around it. They soon discovered that the 'rocks' were actually piles of brick and rubble, clothed in concrete. Things got more exciting when they found steps leading down into the ground. Thank goodness for the Harrises, who have had the courage and imagination to undertake such an ambitious

restoration project. Today the grottoes are clad once again with a convincing mixture of real and artificial rock. Ferns of every description thrive in the damp, green twilight, trailing their fronds in pools of dark water. When the sun shines, it penetrates the grottoes in artful shafts, illuminating the verdant leaves of some lucky fern and throwing the rocky walls into mysterious shadow.

RIGHT This strange creature guards the entrance to the tunnel linking the Fern Grotto to the Tufa Grotto.

LEFT Sunlight illuminates the leaves of a tree fern growing happily among Pulhamite rocks in the grotto garden.

RIGHT Water runs right through the Lion Grotto. Now that it is restored, Dewstow Gardens has received a Grade I listing.

high glanau manor
monmouthshire

High Glanau is a lovely Arts and Crafts house on a wooded hillside above Monmouth. It was designed by Eric Francis of Chepstow for H. Avray Tipping and built between 1918 and 1927. It was the third of three houses that Tipping had owned in Monmouthshire. The first was Mathern Place and the second Mounton, both near Chepstow. Tipping was a restless man, unable to remain in any of his houses after the garden had reached maturity. At High Glanau his tenure was even shorter. He left in 1930 for London, where he died in 1933. His plans for the garden have survived, however, as have several photographs of the house and the garden taken during his lifetime and stored in the archives of *Country Life*. High Glanau is lucky in its present owners, Helena and Hilary Gerrish, who bought the house in 2000. Armed with Tipping's original plans and the photographs, Helena has worked with great gentleness and determination to restore the garden, and under her care it is finally re-emerging from years of misunderstanding and neglect.

Tipping was not a trained architect, but he had spent twenty years or more writing on architecture and gardens for *Country Life*. At High Glanau he collaborated with Eric Francis to achieve perfect integration between house and garden. 'You can't really understand the garden without seeing it from inside the house,' Helena says. This is because Tipping aligned all the main axes of the garden with the windows of the principal rooms. As a result, 'You can't look out of the windows without feeling that you are being swept outside into the garden.' The drawing room overlooks the stone terraces on the west side of the house, and the vast and

wonderful view beyond. Broad stone steps form the central axis, and at the foot of them Tipping made an octagonal stone pool. Below the pool winding paths, as yet largely unrestored, led down into the woods, where he grew shade-loving plants among the trees. This contrast between the formal lines of the terraces and the more natural woodland was one of the effects that Tipping loved to achieve. However, the view from his study on the south side of the house was of perfect order. A broad grass walk flanked by herbaceous borders led to the high stone wall of the kitchen garden. Against the wall Tipping built one of his trademark pergolas.

When the Gerrishes arrived at High Glanau there were hedges growing on the terraces, obscuring the view down to the pool. Now the beds are overflowing with a very soft and English combination of delphiniums, alliums, peonies, poppies and mounds of catmint. Helena has chosen the pink *Rosa* 'Gertrude Jekyll', *R*. 'William Morris' and *R*. 'Charles Rennie Mackintosh' to grow against the walls of the house. Why? Because, like the house, 'they all have Arts and Crafts associations,' she explains. Helena's generous planting is beautifully judged: it counteracts the Italianate austerity of the terraces, re-creating the tension that Tipping would have intended.

The south garden presented more of a challenge. Half of the grass walk had been replaced with a swimming pool, and the pergola at its far end was derelict. It requires conviction to take out a swimming pool but, as Hilary explains, the Gerrishes are determined to protect the future of High Glanau and its garden by restoring it and then 'putting it back on the map so that it can never be forgotten again'.

RIGHT The view back towards Tipping's study window on the south side of the house. The Gerrishes have recently removed the swimming pool that occupied this site, and when the photograph was taken the planting was still in its infancy.

ON PAGES 100–101
At the far end of the upper terrace, formality gives way to the cottage-garden feel of this richly planted space.

RIGHT The acid-green flowers of lady's mantle (*Alchemilla mollis*) froth over the edge of the flower bed and on to the uneven paving slabs, adding to the informal atmosphere at the southern end of the terrace.

llanfihangel court
monmouthshire

Llanfihangel Court is a handsome Tudor manor house built beneath the Skirrid mountain. Little remains of the garden created for John Arnold in the second half of the seventeenth century, but the message it was designed to convey can still be read loud and clear.

Arnold enlarged the simple stone building that he had inherited from his father and added a grand entrance façade to its north side. A generous stone staircase was built to link the new front door to the carriage drive and the lower garden. Visitors approaching the house from this direction would have driven down a long avenue of pines. Their view down the drive was stopped by the house, its imposing bulk anchored to the surrounding landscape by the broad grassy terraces that extend to each side of the central staircase – a composition that broadcasts wealth, power and permanence to this day. The carriage drive is long gone, but Mr and Mrs Johnson, the current owners, have replaced Arnold's short-lived pines and re-created the avenue. The trees are in their infancy, but soon they will march confidently across the field below the house. Arnold also planted an avenue of sweet chestnuts to flank the southern approach. Battered and shattered, some of the trees still stand but, once again, the drive no longer exists. The modern approach to the house is a lane that climbs up and around the building before entering a sunny yard on its east side, where peacocks parade their finery and offer a deafening greeting. From this vantage point the house presents a far less formal face. The narrow space between it and the wall on its west side is occupied by a rectangular lily pool and a wonderful accumulation of plants in the courtyard garden. *Hydrangea petiolaris* and wisteria swathe the mellow walls of the house, and ferns, moss, valerian and lady's mantle (*Alchemilla mollis*) infest the cracks between the stones.

LEFT A peacock above the lily pond in the narrow courtyard on the west side of the house.

llanover house
monmouthshire

a circular dovecote already on the site. Today the dovecote, creeper clad, has its feet in a lavish herbaceous border planted against the wall. The stream forms a still, dark pool enclosing the garden on its other side, where pale pink roses line the bank.

In 1823 Benjamin Waddington's daughter Augusta married to Benjamin Hall, an industrialist and politician, and they made their home at Llanover. In 1838 Hall was made a baronet and Augusta became Lady Llanover. She championed all things Welsh, becoming a patron of Welsh language, literature and customs, and even establishing a definitive design for the Welsh national costume. All the household staff at Llanover, including the resident harpist, were Welsh speaking, and during Augusta's lifetime the estate became a centre for national and international culture. The house hummed with activity, and among the guests wandering in the lovely gardens there were often bards, politicians, musicians, diplomats and members of Europe's royal families.

In 1922 Lord Treowen, Lady Llanover's grandson, planted the stately avenue of sweet chestnuts between the house and the main gate. Narcissi carpet the ground below the trees in spring, but by early May they have given way to sheets of the lovely, lily-flowered tulip 'Red Shine', combined with clouds of cow parsley.

Today Llanover is the home of Elizabeth Murray, a descendant of Lady Llanover. Elizabeth and her husband continue the tradition of tree planting that was begun by Benjamin Waddington at the end of the eighteenth century and continued by her grandparents, Sir John and Lady Mary Herbert, in the 1930s, and her father, Robin Herbert, CBE, who is an ex-President of the Royal Horticultural Society. This continuous regime of planting and renewal has resulted in a remarkable arboretum. Five trees in the collection are registered as 'champions' on the national tree register, among them a magnificent California buckeye (*Aesculus californica*) with a 13-metre/37-foot spread. Memories of a childhood spent partly on the east coast of America inspired Robin Herbert to plant trees renowned for their autumn colour, and by October the garden blazes with the foliage of liquidambars, maples (*Acer* spp.), nyssas and hickories (*Carya* spp.). He has also planted fifteen different varieties of magnolia to flower throughout the spring and summer.

LEFT A stream encloses one side of Llanover's lovely walled garden, and leaves it through this generous, semicircular arch.

The gardens of Llanover House were laid out at the end of the eighteenth century for Benjamin Waddington. The site was ideal for the naturalistic treatment so fashionable at that time. The garden architect's name is unfortunately lost to us, but he made good use of an abundant stream that flowed on to the estate to the north of the house, sending the water into the site through a series of miniature cascades, under bridges, through narrow, fast-flowing rills and over weirs. Water still dominates the garden today. The stream, which is much given to partings and reunions, still winds its way through the garden, bringing light, sound and movement to every part of it. In early summer, the rainbow colours of rhododendrons are reflected in the water.

Waddington's garden was lavishly planted with trees, and some of his fine beeches and towering London planes survive to this day. The unusual circular walled garden built in the eighteenth century is still at the heart of the layout. Its north wall was made to embrace

penpergwm lodge
monmouthshire

When Simon and Catriona Boyle first moved to Penpergwm Lodge in 1976, the house was surrounded by a very plain Edwardian garden and some lovely trees. There was a large, sloping vegetable garden above the house that was enclosed by beech hedges on three sides and a sturdy apple-clad pergola on the fourth. In those early years Catriona was too busy looking after four small children to do much gardening. 'I didn't really get going', she says, 'until I started my garden school. That was when I began to learn about all the lovely plants that are available.'

Catriona was an avid pupil in her own school. 'I have no training myself,' she explains, 'so I always take lots of advice from people with good ideas.' She invited some illustrious tutors to her school, and they were never too shy to express their views about Catriona's own garden. When Helen Dillon saw the potager that the Boyles had made on the site of the old vegetable garden, she said that the slope made her feel 'seasick'. 'When I overheard that,' Simon recalls, 'I knew that the JCB would not be far behind.' How right he was. Before long, the offending slope had been cut into a series of level terraces with brick retaining walls.

Helen Dillon's garden in Dublin was the inspiration for the shallow stepped canal that runs down the centre of the terraces. The Boyles cleverly added black paint to the cement used for lining the canal, and as a result the water acts as a perfect mirror to the flowers growing in beds to either side of it, and the graceful brick loggia that has been designed and built, with Simon's assistance, by James Arbuthnott at the top of the site. James, whose own garden at Stone House Cottage in Worcestershire is

well known for its brick follies, also built the magnificent brick viewing tower that overlooks the terrace garden. Catriona has planted the terraces with a potager mix of flowers and vegetables. 'I suppose everyone likes doing different things,' she says, 'and I loathe planting out hundreds of the same kind of plant.' What Catriona likes is 'mixing combinations of different things', and as a result, the terraces are a constantly changing tapestry of intense colours and contrasting textures. Visit the garden in August, and you will find Catriona tearing out all the midsummer planting to make way for the next set of brilliant ideas. She's never afraid to change her mind, and when Simon watches her embarking on something new he sometimes says to himself, 'How long is this going to last, I wonder?'

New building in the terrace garden has made it the centre of attention, but it is just one of a series of lovely ideas at Penpergwm. There is the graceful, vine-clad pergola in the lower garden, for example, where the delicate flowers of *Clematis* 'Perle d'Azur' appear among the vine leaves in August. Then there is the crab apple avenue, underplanted with crocuses and pheasant's eye daffodils (*Narcissus poeticus* var. *recurvus*), and the box parterre designed by Simon Dorrell on the west side of the house. Catriona has joined forces with Joanna Kerr to run a small nursery at the entrance to the garden, where you can buy unusual herbaceous plants, bulbs, shrubs and half-hardy perennials. Catriona and Joanna also work together to provide the answers to gardening questions posed by readers of *Saga* magazine.

LEFT Seen from the loggia, the steps become almost invisible and the canal looks like a gently flowing stream. The beds to either side are filled with a rich mix of late-summer cutting flowers and vegetables.

RIGHT Mixed herbaceous planting backed by shrubs and trees in a bed behind the house.

BELOW *Clematis* 'Perle d'Azur' twines through the vine leaves on the pergola. This handsome metal framework was made by a local blacksmith, who copied the ogee arch of the apple tunnel that was already on site when the Boyles moved into Penpergwm Lodge.

veddw house
monmouthshire

Veddw House has the most controversial garden in Wales, and that's the way its owners, Ann Wareham and Charles Hawes, like it. They have designed Veddw's garden to break through the culture of bland acceptance that cloaks garden visiting and to provoke discussion. Ann is 'tired of hearing people say how lovely the garden is', and hungry for uninhibited visitors who will criticize her design, inspiring her to refine and develop her ideas.

The object of this focused attention is a garden made behind the house in a shallow valley surrounded by trees, and on the sloping land in front of it. When Ann first moved to Monmouthshire twenty years ago, she knew that she wanted to make a garden, but she wasn't, as yet, much of a gardener. The learning curve was steep. It all began on a day spent with a friend who was a professional designer. 'That taught me what I didn't want to do,' she says, 'and precipitated what I wanted to achieve, and how.' Ann knew that she wanted some formality in the garden, and from this instinct she planted the valley behind the house with an interlocking grid of yew hedges that make a series of enclosed, garden rooms. It is in these rooms that the visitor is first aware that Ann and Charles have not set out merely to create a series of pretty pictures. The pictures are pretty, for the most part, but they have another dimension, a dimension almost entirely lost to the garden some two hundred years ago. Until the mid-eighteenth century it was fashionable to encode the garden with meaning, using it to convey social, political, religious or aesthetic ideas. Yves Arbrioux, a French philosopher, observed that the contemporary garden has been 'reduced to muteness'. Not so at the Veddw.

Ann did not set out to make a 'conceptual' garden. It evolved from her experience of moving to Monmouthshire. Having grown up in Yorkshire, she found the landscape 'alien and strange'. She countered this feeling by studying local history, and gradually she began to experience some sense of belonging. 'What I began to understand about the history of the place,' she explains, 'worked its way backwards into the design, and found expression in the garden.' Local history and the geography of the Monmouthshire landscape became the themes of the garden. There is the gate to the beech woods, for example, which supports a wooden panel

inscribed with nineteenth-century quotations about the area. Then there is the bench at the top of the garden, where all the different names that have been given to the Veddw over the years are recorded, reflecting the 'English–Welsh muddle' that Ann observed during her research in local archives and the National Library of Wales.

History is also the theme of the grass parterre. This is a semi-circular area divided by box hedges. The lines of the hedges represent the field boundaries recorded on the 1848 tithe map of the area, and the grasses planted between them echo the fields of the real landscape surrounding the garden.

The natural landscape is a constant presence at the Veddw, and never more so than in the Hedge Garden. Here Ann and Charles have planted the hedges one behind the other, clipping them so that they both reflect the undulating shapes of the Monmouthshire hills and are contained exactly within the boundary of the black reflecting pool beside the pink, wave-form bench at the bottom of the garden enclosure.

RIGHT Sculpting the forms in the Hedge Garden was a complex, two-man job, although one of those men was a woman, of course. The apparently free-flowing forms of the hedges were minutely adjusted so that the entire structure would be accurately contained within the confines of the reflecting pool (as can be seen on pages 116–17).

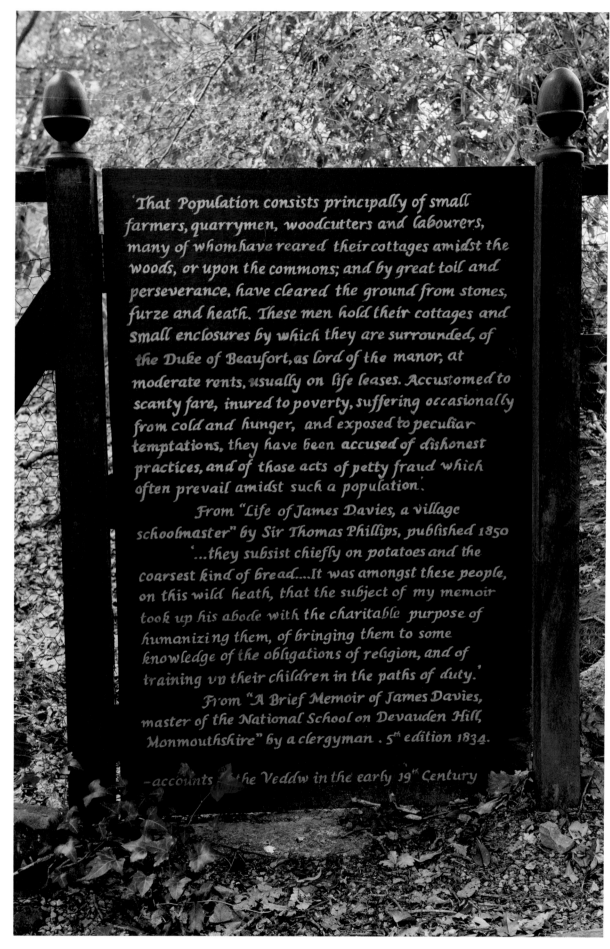

'That Population consists principally of small farmers, quarrymen, woodcutters and labourers, many of whom have reared their cottages amidst the woods, or upon the commons; and by great toil and perseverance, have cleared the ground from stones, furze and heath. These men hold their cottages and small enclosures by which they are surrounded, of the Duke of Beaufort, as lord of the manor, at moderate rents, usually on life leases. Accustomed to scanty fare, inured to poverty, suffering occasionally from cold and hunger, and exposed to peculiar temptations, they have been accused of dishonest practices, and of those acts of petty fraud which often prevail amidst such a population'.

From "Life of James Davies, a village schoolmaster" by Sir Thomas Phillips, published 1850

'...they subsist chiefly on potatoes and the coarsest kind of bread....It was amongst these people, on this wild heath, that the subject of my memoir took up his abode with the charitable purpose of humanizing them, of bringing them to some knowledge of the obligations of religion, and of training up their children in the paths of duty.'

From "A Brief Memoir of James Davies, master of the National School on Devauden Hill, Monmouthshire" by a clergyman . 5ᵗʰ edition 1834.

—accounts of the Veddw in the early 19ᵗʰ Century

LEFT Ann forged her relationship with the local landscape by delving deep into its history. During her research she uncovered these nineteenth-century descriptions of the local inhabitants and she has inscribed them on the Population Gate, which marks the boundary between the wood and the garden.

RIGHT, ABOVE A view from above, across the jigsaw of interlocking hedges. A ribbon of copper beech runs through the beech hedge in the foreground, creating a wonderful effect.

RIGHT, BELOW The Veddw demands a response. If the clever and articulate spaces of the main garden leave you cold, the discovery of this nasty plastic chair and television in the beautiful, cathedral-like space made by magisterial beeches on the edge of the garden is bound to arouse some emotion – and it might even be rage.

ON PAGES 116–17 There is a concrete seat on the edge of the water, and this is the perfect viewpoint from which to enjoy the maze of undulating hedges reflected in the inky water of the pool.

wyndcliffe court
monmouthshire

Wyndcliffe Court is an Arts and Crafts house designed by Eric Francis and built for Charles Clay in 1922. Clay commissioned H. Avray Tipping to design a garden to the south and west of the house. Francis and Tipping were used to collaborating, for Francis was the architect of two of Tipping's own houses. Their familiarity is evident at Wyndcliffe, where house and garden sit happily together. The garden, with its toppling yew topiary, sun-warmed-stone walls, formal terracing, trickling fountain and bowling-green lawn, bears all the hallmarks of Tipping's designs. It is a much larger garden than Tipping's own at High Glanau, but it has the same generous proportions and comfortable, domestic feel. It is a place designed for carefree family life and relaxed entertaining.

The house stands above a broad south-facing terrace, where capsizing mounds of clipped yew jostle among stone-edged flowerbeds and water drips from an elegant dolphin wall fountain. Wind is an issue in this garden, and the shelterbelt that Tipping planted below the terraces has reached a gigantic height, effectively cutting much of the garden off from a spectacular view across open countryside to the Bristol Channel. However, the interface between the smooth grass of the bowling green below the terrace gives way to shady paths through the woods, creating exactly the contrast between cultivation and natural landscape that Tipping loved.

From the west end of the terrace the view is crowded with wonderfully uneven topiary forms. Beyond them is the sunken garden, a suntrap with sides cut into shallow terraces and an elegant, stone lily pond at its centre. A summerhouse stands on the south-west corner of the sunken garden, overlooking it, the vegetable and cutting garden and a view through the shelterbelt to the south. The last Mrs Clay made sure that the trees were cut to frame the view from the summerhouse to the Bristol Channel, but Mr and Mrs Clay died a few years ago and the trees have already begun to create a screen. Inside the garden, however, Ken Brooking, who was the Clays' gardener, wages a miraculously successful battle against the forces of nature. It is hard to imagine how he manages to keep this large garden, topiary included, in such good heart.

ABOVE Warm stone terraces, bulging topiary and a good splash of colour. The garden of Wyndcliffe Court bears all the hallmarks of a Tipping design.

RIGHT, ABOVE There are still some vegetables grown in the walled garden, but it is drifts of flowers that fill it with life and colour.

RIGHT, BELOW Quirky topiary shapes crowd the narrow terraces.

BELOW Ornate wrought-iron
gates at the entrance to the
walled garden.

BELOW The view across the
sunken garden to the
summerhouse, designed by
Eric Francis, where Mrs Clay
used to enjoy a view cut
through the trees towards the
Bristol Channel.

south glamorgan

dyffryn gardens
cardiff

What a lovely surprise Dyffryn is. If you went there before 1997, you must go back. Since then, the 55-acre/22-hectare garden that was designed by Thomas Mawson in 1906 has been the focus of an extraordinarily successful restoration project. Colin Sharp, senior gardener, has worked at Dyffryn for twenty-two years. He remembers the bad old days, when low staffing levels obliged the gardeners to be selective about maintenance, and many parts of the garden were too dilapidated to open to the public. What a difference a decade of funding from Heritage Lottery and the local authority makes. Today the entire garden glows with wellbeing, and visitors are free to explore thirty-three different areas in Mawson's wonderfully complex design. And it doesn't stop there. The next phase, the restoration of the walled kitchen garden and the glasshouses, is already under way.

Mawson was engaged by Reginald Cory to re-model the garden surrounding his father's late Victorian mansion. Cory was quite a plantsman and designer in his own right. He became Vice President of the Royal Horticultural Society and gave generously to many horticultural causes, including the Cambridge Botanic Garden. He also funded several expeditions for plant hunters such as George Forrest, 'Chinese' Wilson and Reginald Farrer. This link greatly enriched the planting of the garden. Among the trees in the Arboretum, for example, there is a paper bark maple (*Acer griseum*), a native of China that is thought to have been grown from a seed brought back to England for the first time by 'Chinese' Wilson, and is certainly the largest tree of its kind in Britain. Between 1913 and 1914, Cory organized dahlia trials at Dyffryn. The trials included over three thousand plants, and Cory is credited with saving the dahlia from oblivion and preserving it as a decorative plant.

Mawson and Cory worked closely together. Mawson designed the layout, but Cory was in charge of planting. Mawson recalls the freedom of their collaboration in his *Art and Craft of Garden Making*, an extremely popular book that ran into five editions: 'We felt at liberty to indulge in every phase of garden design which the site and my client's catholic views suggested.' On the south side of the house he made a magnificent balustraded terrace. Below it the parterre beds of the original Victorian garden were retained. Today these parterres are packed with a colourful, surprising and supremely successful combination of bedding plants. 'We used to do a fairly standard bedding scheme here,' Colin Sharp remarks, 'but in 2006, the garden's centenary, we decided to do some research into Edwardian bedding schemes'. Cordylines had also been an important feature in this part of the garden during the 1920s, and in 2006 the Friends of Dyffryn Gardens re-created history when they donated the cordylines that form the centrepieces of the parterres today. Not all the plants used in the beds would have been available to Edwardian gardeners, but the exuberant spirit of the original garden is there. Mawson extended the garden on the south side with a formal canal punctuated by a lily pond that has a fountain at its centre.

In 1905 Mawson and Cory went on a garden visiting expedition to Italy. The influence of this journey is felt in a dense network of garden rooms that Mawson designed to the west of the house. At the top of the site, next to the walled garden, however, the atmosphere is intensely English. Two broad herbaceous borders are enclosed on one side by the wall of the kitchen garden and on the other by concrete columns linked by metal arches. These beds were once a showcase for Cory's collection of unusual and exotic plants, and some plants from his original scheme survive. Among these is the tender, evergreen Macartney rose (*Rosa bracteata*) and a *Crinodendron hookerianum*, which is thought to be the same specimen that Cory originally grew in a tub beside the glasshouses. The beds are beautifully and imaginatively planted today with the same generosity and panache as the parterres in front of the house.

Below the herbaceous borders Mawson created a series of wonderful gardens separated by yew hedges, walls or arches that also serve to frame enticing views through the garden, arousing the curiosity of visitors and drawing them on. Among the many rooms there is an Italian terrace, a theatre garden, a reflecting pool garden, where the colossal, blue heads of agapanthus are mirrored in the water, a cloister made from yew hedges and said to be designed by Cory himself, and, most extraordinary of all, the Pompeiian Garden. Here Mawson took his inspiration from the gardens excavated at Pompeii. A circular fountain marks its centre, and wisteria grows up the colonnade.

LEFT, ABOVE Looking towards the house across the Great Lawn and the Water Lily Canal.

LEFT, BELOW Maples colour up for autumn in the arboretum, where the collection includes fourteen champion trees

All information was correct at the time of going to press, but it is advisable to check opening times before visiting the gardens.

The Yellow Book lists around 3,500 gardens, mostly private, that open to the public for charity under the National Gardens Scheme (www.ngs.org.uk). It is published annually.

GWYNEDD

Bodysgallen Hall, Llandudno, Caernarfonshire
LL30 IRS
01492 584466, www.bodysgallen.com
Bodysgallen is a hotel and the garden is open
to guests

Plas Brondanw, Croesor, Llanfrothen, Caernarfonshire
LL48 6SW
01766 770000/01743 241181, www.brondanw.org
Open daily 9.30 a.m.–5.30 p.m. all year round

Plas Newydd, Llanfairpwll, Anglesey LL61 6DQ
01248 714795, www.nationaltrust.org.uk
Open mid-March to end of October,
10.30 a.m.–5.30 p.m.; closed Thursday and Friday

Plas yn Rhiw, Rhiw, Pwllheli Lleyn Peninsula LL53 8AB
01758 780219, www.nationaltrust.org.uk
Open end of March to beginning of November;
opening times vary

Crûg Farm Plants, Griffith's Crossing, Caernarfon,
Caernarfonshire LL55 1TU
01248 670232, info@crug-farm.co.uk
Open March–June: Thursday–Sunday,
10.00 a.m.–5.00 p.m. and Bank Holidays;
July–September: Thursday–Saturday,
10.00 a.m.–5.00 p.m., closed for Bank Holidays

CLWYD

Bodnant Garden, Tal-y-Cafn, Colwyn Bay, Conwy
LL28 5RE
01492 650460, www.bodnantgarden.co.uk
Open March–November, 10.00 a.m.–5.00 p,m; last
admission 4.30 p.m.

Bodrhyddan Hall, Rhuddlan, Denbighshire LL18 5SB
Lord and Lady Langford, 01745 590414,
www.bodrhyddan.co.uk
Open June–September, Tuesdays and Thursdays,
2.00–5.30 p.m.

Chirk Castle, Chirk, Denbighshire LL14 5AF
01691 777701, www.nationaltrust.org.uk
Opening times vary throughout the year

Erddig, Wrexham, Denbighshire LL13 0YT
01978 315151, www.nationaltrust.org.uk
Opening times vary throughout the year

POWYS

Llowes Court, Llowes, Hay-on-Wye, Brecknockshire
HR3 5JA
Mr and Mrs Briggs, 01497 847882
Open for *The Yellow Book*

Powis Castle, Welshpool, Montgomeryshire SY21 8RF
01938 551994, www.nationaltrust.org.uk
Open beginning of March to end of November;
opening times vary

DYFED

Aberglasney, Llangathen, Carmarthenshire SA32 8QH
01558 668998, www.aberglasney.org
Open summer (April–September)
10.00 a.m.–6.00 p.m., last entry 5.00 p.m.;
winter (October–March) 10.30 a.m.–4.00 p.m.,
last entry 3.00 p.m.

Cae Hir Gardens, Cribyn, Lampeter, Ceredigion
SA48 7NG
Wil Akkermans, 01570 470839,
www.caehirgardens.ws
Open 1.00 p.m.–6.00 p.m. daily except Sundays;
open Bank Holidays. Open by appointment only
outside these hours. Groups welcome

The Cilwendeg Shell House, Cilwendeg, Boncath,
Pembrokeshire SA37 0EW
For information, contact the Temple Trust,
0207 482 6171

Ffynone, Boncath, Pembrokeshire SA37 0HQ
Earl and Countess Lloyd George, 01239 841610
Open in spring for *The Yellow Book*

Llanllyr, Talsarn, Lampeter, Ceredigion SA48 8QB
Mr and Mrs Robert Gee, 01570 470900
Open for *The Yellow Book* and by appointment

The National Botanic Garden of Wales, Llanarthne,
Carmarthenshire SA32 8HG
01558 667148/9, www.gardenofwales.org.uk
Open daily, apart from Christmas Day:
28 October – 30 March 10.00 a.m.–4.30 p.m.;
31 March – 26 October 10.00 a.m.–6.00 p.m.

Picton Castle, Haverfordwest, SA62 4AS
01437 751326, www.pictoncastle.co.uk
Open Easter–end of September: Tuesday–Sunday,
closed Mondays except Bank Holidays,
10.30am–5.00pm; castle tours 11.30 a.m.–3.30 p.m.
October: castle, galleries, gardens and restaurant
open weekends; gardens only mid-week
Winter: gardens only open, seven days a week,
10.30 a.m.–dusk

Rhos-y-gilwen Mansion, North Pembrokeshire
SA43 2TW
01239 841 387, www.rhosygilwen.co.uk
Open for events or by appointment

GWENT

Clytha Park, Clytha, Abergavenny, Monmouthshire
NP7 9BW
Sir Richard Hanbury-Tenison, 01873 840300
Open for *The Yellow Book*

Dewstow Gardens and Grottoes, Caerwent,
Monmouthshire NP26 5AH
01291 430444, www.dewstow.co.uk
Open 10.00 a.m.–4.00 p.m.

High Glanau, Lydart, Monmouth, Monmouthshire
NP25 4AD
Mr and Mrs H. Gerrish, 01600 860 005
Open for *The Yellow Book*

Llanfihangel Court, Llanfihangel Crucorney,
Abergavenny, Monmouthshire NP7 8DH
Mr and Mrs D. Johnson, 01873 890217
Open strictly by appointment

Llanover House, Llanover, Abergavenny,
Monmouthshire NP7 9EF
Mr and Mrs M.R. Murray, 01873 880232,
www.llanover.com
Open for *The Yellow Book*

Penpergwm Lodge, Abergavenny, Monmouthshire
NP7 9AS
01873 840208, www.penplants.com
Open April–September, Thursday–Sunday,
2.00–6.00 p.m.

Veddw House, Devauden, Monmouthshire,
NP16 6PH
Ann Wareham and Charles Hawes, 01291 650836,
www.veddw.co.uk
Open 1 June–31 August inclusive, Sundays and
Bank Holidays, 2.00 p.m.–5.00 p.m.

Wyndcliffe Court, St Arvans, Nr Chepstow,
Monmouthshire NP16 6EY
01291 622352
Open only by appointment

SOUTH GLAMORGAN

Dyffryn Gardens, St Nicholas, Vale of Glamorgan,
CF5 6SU
029 2059 3328, www.dyffryngardens.org.uk
Open March 11.00 a.m.–4.00 p.m.; April–October
10.00 a.m.–6.00 p.m.; November–February
11.00–4.00 p.m. (closed Tuesday and Wednesday)

index